Common Core Language Arts Workouts Grade 8

AUTHOR: Linda Armstrong
EDITOR: Mary Dieterich
PROOFREADER: Margaret Brown

COPYRIGHT © 2015 Mark Twain Media, Inc.

ISBN 978-1-62223-525-4

Printing No. CD-404228

Mark Twain Media, Inc., Publishers
Distributed by Carson-Dellosa Publishing LLC

Visit us at www.carsondellosa.com

Table of Contents
With Common Core State Standards Correlations

Table of Contents
With Common Core State Standards Correlations (cont.)

Table of Contents
With Common Core State Standards Correlations (cont.)

Table of Contents
With Common Core State Standards Correlations (cont.)

Table of Contents
With Common Core State Standards Correlations (cont.)

Table of Contents
With Common Core State Standards Correlations (cont.)

CCSS.ELA-LITERACY.L.8.3.A: Use verbs in the active and passive voice and in the conditional and subjunctive mood to achieve particular effects (e.g., emphasizing the actor or the action; expressing uncertainty or describing a state contrary to fact).

Vocabulary Acquisition and Use

CCSS.ELA-LITERACY.L.8.4: Determine or clarify the meaning of unknown and multiple-meaning words or phrases based on Grade 8 reading and content, choosing flexibly from a range of strategies.
CCSS.ELA-LITERACY.L.8.4.A: Use context (e.g., the overall meaning of a sentence or paragraph; a word's position or function in a sentence) as a clue to the meaning of a word or phrase.

CCSS.ELA-LITERACY.L.8.4.B: Use common, grade-appropriate Greek or Latin affixes and roots as clues to the meaning of a word (e.g., *precede, recede, secede*).

CCSS.ELA-LITERACY.L.8.4.C: Consult general and specialized reference materials (e.g., dictionaries, glossaries, thesauruses), both print and digital, to find the pronunciation of a word or determine or clarify its precise meaning or its part of speech.
CCSS.ELA-LITERACY.L.8.4.D: Verify the preliminary determination of the meaning of a word or phrase (e.g., by checking the inferred meaning in context or in a dictionary).

CCSS.ELA-LITERACY.L.8.5: Demonstrate understanding of figurative language, word relationships, and nuances in word meanings.
CCSS.ELA-LITERACY.L.8.5.A: Interpret figures of speech (e.g. verbal irony, puns) in context.

CCSS.ELA-LITERACY.L.8.5.B: Use the relationship between particular words to better understand each of the words.
CCSS.ELA-LITERACY.L.8.5.C: Distinguish among the connotations (associations) of words with similar denotations (definitions) (e.g., *bullheaded, willful, firm, persistent, resolute*).

CCSS.ELA-LITERACY.L.8.6: Acquire and use accurately grade-appropriate general academic and domain-specific words and phrases; gather vocabulary knowledge when considering a word or phrase important to comprehension or expression.

* Skills and understandings that are particularly likely to require continued attention in higher grades as they are applied to increasingly sophisticated writing and speaking are marked with an asterisk (*).

Introduction to the Teacher

The time has come to make our children's reading, writing, and speaking education more rigorous. The Common Core State Standards were developed for this purpose. They guide educators and parents by outlining the skills students are expected to master at each grade level. The bar has been set high, but with a little help, students can meet the challenge.

Common Core Language Arts Workouts, Grade 8 is designed to assist teachers and parents who are implementing the new requirements. It is filled with skills practice pages, critical-thinking tasks, and creative exercises that correspond to each standard for language arts.

Each day, students will work with a different grade-level-specific language arts skill. The brief exercises will challenge them to read, think, and speak with improved facility.

Every page contains at least one "workout." The workouts vary according to the standard covered. Some are simple practice exercises. Others pose creative or analytical challenges. Certain pages invite further exploration. Suggested student projects include reports, speeches, discussions, and multimedia presentations.

The workout pages make great warm-up or assessment exercises. They can set the stage and teach the content covered by the standards. They can also be used to assess what students have learned after the content has been taught.

We hope that the ideas and exercises in this book will help you work more effectively with the Common Core State Standards. The series also includes books for Grade 6 and Grade 7. With your help, we are confident that students will develop increased language arts power and become more effective communicators!

Name: _____ Date: _____

READING LITERATURE: KEY IDEAS AND DETAILS—
Understanding the Text

CCSS.ELA-LITERACY.RL.8.1: Cite the textual evidence that most strongly supports an analysis of what the text says explicitly as well as inferences drawn from the text.

Directions: Read the selection and then answer the questions.

Bad Day on Route 22

A disheveled man slightly north of 40 stumbled into the roadside café. It was a little past noon and all the stools at the counter were occupied by truckers and loggers. They were concentrating on their sandwiches and coffee so they didn't notice when the new-comer collapsed into the too-soft red cushions of a corner booth, grimacing slightly.

Eileen noticed though, it was her job to monitor everyone and everything that came through that door, especially after the call she had just received from Pete, the head ranger out at the national park. This character matched his description perfectly.

Eileen glanced back at the man before slipping through the swinging doors into the kitchen. The plates on her tray jiggled.

Jake stopped flipping a pancake and studied her curiously. "Shaky this morning, eh?"

Eileen shook her head, set the tray down, and then headed for the phone on the wall by the sink.

---

1. Does this story take place in the desert, the mountains, or the city? Which details in the selection let you know?

   _____

   _____

   _____

2. How does Eileen feel about the disheveled man who has just entered the café? Which details in the selection let you know?

   _____

   _____

   _____

3. Who is Jake? Which details in the selection let you know?

   _____

   _____

4. What was Eileen planning to do?

   _____

   _____

Name: _____   Date: _____

READING LITERATURE: KEY IDEAS AND DETAILS—
Fiction Analysis Record Sheet

CCSS.ELA-LITERACY.RL.8.2: Determine a theme or central idea of a text and analyze its development over the course of the text, including its relationship to the characters, setting, and plot; provide an objective summary of the text.

Directions: Read a short story or novel. Fill in the information below.

Title: _____

Author: _____

Theme (coming-of-age, man against nature, greed, love, friendship, perseverance, patience, individuality, courage, gratitude, etc.): _____

Viewpoint character or characters (narrator): _____

Narrative Point of View (first-, second-, or third-person?): _____

Main character (protagonist): _____

Main character's problem (What does he or she want?): _____

_____

_____

_____

Main character's flaw (examples: fear, pride, greed, envy, too trusting): _____

Villain or Opposing Force (antagonist): _____

Villain's problem (What does he or she want?): _____

_____

_____

Villain's flaw: _____

How is the main character's problem related to the story's central idea or theme?

_____

_____

_____

Setting (time and place): _____

How does the setting contribute to the theme? _____

_____

In a few sentences, explain what this novel or story is about. _____

_____

_____

_____

Name: _____   Date: _____

READING LITERATURE: KEY IDEAS AND DETAILS—
Analyzing Dialogue

CCSS.ELA-LITERACY.RL.8.3: Analyze how particular lines of dialogue or incidents in a story or drama propel the action, reveal aspects of a character, or provoke a decision.

Directions: Read the selection. Answer the questions.

> Martin put a finger to his lips. "Shh! I think he's coming back."
>
> Angel nodded. The darkened dining hall was eerily quiet. A lingering aroma of macaroni and cheese blended with the sharp scent of pine disinfectant. A wave of nausea swept over Angel, but he took a deep breath and it passed. Around them, legs of chairs stacked upside down on table tops loomed like bizarre metal antennae.
>
> Angel felt someone poke him in the back and involuntarily jumped. His pounding heart slowed a little when he heard Robin's trembling voice. "What will Mr. Collins do when he finds out we aren't in the dormitory?"
>
> Angel shook his head.
>
> Insistent, Robin tugged at the arm of his sweatshirt. "But Angel, what will he do?"
>
> "Robin, think! What's going to happen if he hears you?" Martin glared at the terrified third-grader.
>
> Angel pulled his brother down with one hand, covering the boy's mouth with the other. The trio crouched behind a counter and waited.
>
> The school's headmaster strode down the hallway. When his footsteps receded, Martin stood up cautiously and looked around. "We have to get out of here."

1. How do the boys feel? _____ How do you know? _____
   _____

2. Who is in charge? _____ How do you know? _____
   _____

3. Who is the viewpoint character? _____ How do you know? _____
   _____

4. The word "said" does not appear in this passage. How does the writer let you know who is speaking? Give an example. _____
   _____
   _____

5. Which character do you like the best? Why? _____
   _____
   _____

Challenge: On another paper, analyze a page of dialogue from a novel or short story. Explain how each character's dialogue reveals his personality or motivates action.

Name: _____ Date: _____

READING LITERATURE: CRAFT AND STRUCTURE—
Using Context to Understand Vocabulary

CCSS.ELA-LITERACY.RL.8.4: Determine the meaning of words and phrases as they are used in a text, including figurative and connotative meanings; analyze the impact of specific word choices on meaning and tone, including analogies or allusions to other texts.

Directions: Read the verse. Answer the questions.

An Old Lady From Breen

There was an old lady from Breen
Who was astoundingly clean.
She was quite meticulous
In fact so ridiculous
She scoured snowflakes and air in between.

1. What does *meticulous* mean? _____

2. What does *ridiculous* mean? _____

3. What does *astoundingly* mean? _____

4. What does *scoured* mean? _____

5. What is the tone of this verse? (Examples: serious, angry, humorous, romantic)

_____

6. How does the writer's choice of vocabulary help to establish the tone of the verse?

_____

_____

7. What is the form of this verse? (Examples: couplet, limerick, sonnet, ballad, ode)

_____

8. What is ridiculous about her actions in the last line? _____

_____

_____

Challenge: Read "The New Colossus" by Emma Lazarus (available online.) On another paper, compare the poem's form, tone, and vocabulary to their counterparts in the verse above. Explain the meaning of each of the following phrases: "brazen giant of Greek fame," "storied pomp," "tempest-tost," and "mighty woman with a torch." In the line that begins "Keep ancient lands…" who is being quoted?

Name: _____ Date: _____

READING LITERATURE: CRAFT AND STRUCTURE—
Different Forms, Different Purposes

CCSS.ELA-LITERACY.RL.8.5: Compare and contrast the structure of two or more texts and analyze how the differing structure of each text contributes to its meaning and style.

Directions: Read the selections. Write a short paragraph to answer each question.

Selection 1

The Star Spangled Banner (Verse 1)

O say, can you see, by the dawn's early light,
What so proudly we hailed at the twilight's last gleaming?
Whose broad stripes and bright stars, through the perilous fight,
O'er the ramparts we watched, were so gallantly streaming!
And the rockets' red glare, the bombs bursting in air,
Gave proof through the night that our flag was still there:
O say, does that star-spangled banner yet wave
O'er the land of the free and the home of the brave?

Frances Scott Key

Selection 2

The actual Star-Spangled Banner was one of two flags commissioned by Major George Armistead when he assumed command of Fort McHenry in Baltimore. The famed hand-crafted banner was colossal. It measured 30' x 42'. Designed to fly from atop a 90-foot pole, the flag's enormous size enabled observers to spot it from far away. Following specifications established by the Second Flag Act of January 13, 1794, it had 15 stars and 15 stripes.

---

1. What is the purpose of each selection? _____

   _____

   _____

   _____

2. How does the language of each selection contribute to its purpose? _____

   _____

   _____

   _____

3. How does the form and style of each selection contribute to its purpose? ___

   _____

   _____

   _____

Name: _____ Date: _____

READING LITERATURE: CRAFT AND STRUCTURE—
All the World Is a Stage

CCSS.ELA-LITERACY.RL.8.6: Analyze how differences in the points of view of the characters and the audience or reader (e.g., created through the use of dramatic irony) create such effects as suspense or humor.
CCSS.ELA-LITERACY.RL.8.7: Analyze the extent to which a filmed or live production of a story or drama stays faithful to or departs from the text or script, evaluating the choices made by the director or actors.

Directions: View a live or filmed version of *Romeo and Juliet* by William Shakespeare. Then read the original play. Compare the two. Answer the following questions on another paper.

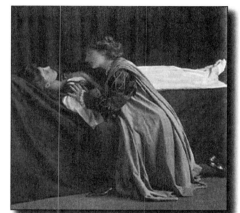

1. How did physical elements such as props, sets, and costumes enhance or change the experience?

2. How did special effects such as stage lighting and sound affect the experience?

3. How did the performances of the actors affect the experience?

4. Were any of the actors too old or too young for their parts? If so, how did this affect the meaning of the play?

5. What was left out of the live or film version, if anything? Did omissions change the meaning of the play? If so, in what ways? If the play was not cut, was it too long? What could have been cut without changing the meaning?

6. When the play opens, what does the audience know about Romeo and Juliet that the characters do not know?

7. When Juliet is standing on her balcony talking about Romeo, what does the audience know that she does not? How does that affect the impact of the scene?

8. Describe another scene from the play when the audience knows something the characters do not know. (This is called dramatic irony.)

Challenge:
1. Using the first five questions above, compare any novel or short story to its film version.
2. In a television comedy or mystery episode, find an example of dramatic irony. What does the audience know that the characters do not? What does this add to the effect of the story?

Name: _____ Date: _____

READING LITERATURE: CRAFT AND STRUCTURE—
Modern Fiction Based on Mythology: Teacher Resources

CCSS.ELA-LITERACY.RL.8.9: Analyze how a modern work of fiction draws on themes, patterns of events, or character types from myths, traditional stories, or religious works such as the Bible, including describing how the material is rendered new.

Possible Fiction Selections

- *The Mark of Athena, The Lightning Thief,* and *The Battle of the Labyrinth* by Rick Riordan (various mythological characters and elements such as Titan, Kronos, and the Labyrinth)
- *The Hunger Games* by Suzanne Collins (Theseus and the Minotaur)
- *Orphans of Chaos* by John C. Wright (various mythological characters)
- *The Fault in Our Stars* by John Green (Sisyphus)
- *Frankenstein: The Modern Prometheus* by Mary Shelley (Prometheus)
- *His Dark Materials* (series) by Philip Pullman (Biblical references and Milton's "Paradise Lost")
- *Alice's Adventures in Wonderland* by Lewis Carroll (Psyche)
- *Till We Have Faces* by C.S. Lewis (Cupid or Eros and Psyche)
- *Goddess of Yesterday: A Tale of Troy* by Caroline B. Cooney (Helen of Troy)
- *Starcrossed* by Josephine Angelini (Helen of Troy and the Furies)
- *Abandon* by Meg Cabot (Persephone)
- *The Maze Runner* by James Dasher (The Labyrinth)
- *The Labours of Hercules* (short story collection) by Agatha Christie (Hercules)

Suggested Questions
1. Summarize the original myth or myths in a few sentences.
2. How is the novel similar to the myth?
3. How does the novel differ from the myth?
4. What is the theme of the myth?
5. Is the theme of the novel the same or different from the theme of the myth?

Name: _____   Date: _____

READING LITERATURE: RANGE OF READING AND LEVEL OF TEXT COMPLEXITY

CCSS.ELA-LITERACY.RL.8.10: By the end of the year, read and comprehend literature, including stories, dramas, and poems, at the high end of Grades 6–8 text complexity band independently and proficiently.

Eighth-Grade Short Stories

Ray Bradbury, "A Sound of Thunder"
Ray Bradbury, "The World the Children Made" (The Veldt)
Anton Chekhov, "The Bet"
Robert Cormier, "The Mustache"
Richard Connell, "The Most Dangerous Game"
Nathaniel Hawthorne, "Doctor Heidegger's Experiment"
Franz Kafka, "The Metamorphosis"
Daniel Keyes, "Flowers for Algernon"
Shirley Jackson, "The Lottery"
W.W. Jacobs, "The Monkey's Paw"
Jack London, "To Build a Fire"
H. H. Munro (Saki), "The Open Window"
Walter Dean Myers, "Jeremiah's Song"
Edgar Allan Poe, "The Fall of the House of Usher"
Edgar Allan Poe, "The Telltale Heart"
Edgar Allan Poe, "The Black Cat"
Laurence Yep, "We Are All One"

Eighth-Grade Novels

Lewis Carroll, *Alice's Adventures in Wonderland* and *Through the Looking-Glass*
Charles Dickens, *A Christmas Carol*
Lois Lowry, *The Giver*
S.E. Hinton, *The Outsiders*
Harper Lee, *To Kill a Mockingbird*
Karen Hesse, *Out of the Dust*
John Steinbeck, *Of Mice and Men*

Eighth-Grade Poems

Online Collections:
"Poetry 180: A Poem a Day for American High Schools"
http://www.loc.gov/poetry/180/003.html
"The EServer Poetry Collection"
http://poetry.eserver.org/

Eighth-Grade Plays

Oscar Wilde, *The Importance of Being Earnest, A Trivial Comedy for Serious People*
Thornton Wilder, *Our Town*
William Shakespeare, *Romeo and Juliet* and *Macbeth*

Name: _____   Date: _____

READING INFORMATIONAL TEXT: KEY IDEAS AND DETAILS—Facts and Inferences

CCSS.ELA-LITERACY.RI.8.1: Cite the textual evidence that most strongly supports an analysis of what the text says explicitly as well as inferences drawn from the text.
CCSS.ELA-LITERACY.RI.8.2: Determine a central idea of a text and analyze its development over the course of the text, including its relationship to supporting ideas; provide an objective summary of the text.

Directions: Read the selection. Answer the questions.

Jedediah Smith

Jedediah Smith was a mountain man. Born in 1799 to a pioneer family, Smith spent his life roaming the formidable mountains and deserts of the Western wilderness. As a teen he was purportedly transfixed by the journals of Lewis and Clark.

When he was 22, Smith joined a trapping expedition led by General William Ashley to collect beaver pelts along the Missouri River. The next year he led a similar expedition into the Rocky Mountains. Later he traversed sweltering deserts to reach territories that later became the states of Arizona and California.

1. In what year did Smith join his first expedition? _____

2. What animals did General William Ashley hunt? _____

3. What was the purpose of Jedediah Smith's expedition into the Rocky Mountains?
   _____

4. How do you think customers used the product Smith brought back from his expeditions?
   _____

5. Is the author sure that Jedediah Smith was inspired by the journals of Lewis and Clark?
   Explain your answer. _____
   _____

6. What is the central idea of this selection? _____
   _____

7. List three facts that support the central idea.
   a. _____
   b. _____
   c. _____

Challenge: The Lewis and Clark Expedition left the shore of the Mississippi River on May 14th, 1804. Read the entries from their journals for the first seven days on the Project Gutenberg site. Then answer the questions on another paper.
  1. What hazards did the group face during the first few days?
  2. What problems did Lewis and Clark have with other members of the expedition?

Name: _____   Date: _____

READING INFORMATIONAL TEXT: KEY IDEAS AND DETAILS—Connections and Distinctions

CCSS.ELA-LITERACY.RI.8.3: Analyze how a text makes connections among and distinctions between individuals, ideas, or events (e.g., through comparisons, analogies, or categories).

Directions: Read the selection. Then answer the questions.

Frances Scott Key and the Star-Spangled Banner

On August 24, 1814 a physician named William Beanes was taken prisoner by the British. At the time, the United States and Great Britain were at war. In fact, the good doctor was seized when the English captured Washington, D.C., and burned the White House.

Francis Scott Key was a prominent lawyer. Though, because of religious beliefs, he opposed the war, Key loved his country. When the American government asked him to negotiate with the British for the doctor's release, he readily agreed. On September 5, he sailed out to the British flagship, *HMS Tonnant,* which was anchored in Baltimore Harbor. Colonel John Skinner, a prisoner exchange agent for the American government, accompanied him in the sloop.

Though the negotiations were successful and Dr. Beanes was released, the trio was not allowed to return to the city that night. The British bombarded Fort McHenry for 25 hours, but were unable to destroy it. In the morning, inspired by the sight of the flag waving over the beleaguered fort, Key scribbled down a poem. It began, "O say can you see…"

1. How did Frances Scott Key feel about the war? Why? _____
   _____

2. Why did Frances Scott Key go to the *HMS Tonnant*? _____
   _____

3. How did he get from the shore to the ship? _____

4. Who was Colonel John Skinner, and why did he accompany Key? _____
   _____
   _____

5. Why were the British bombarding Fort McHenry? _____
   _____

6. Why was the sight of the flag important to Key and the other Americans on the ship?
   _____

7. Would the British aboard the ship have felt the same way about the flag? Why or why not?
   _____
   _____

Name: _____ Date: _____

READING INFORMATIONAL TEXT: CRAFT AND STRUCTURE—
Building Vocabulary Through Context

CCSS.ELA-LITERACY.RI.8.4: Determine the meaning of words and phrases as they are used in a text, including figurative, connotative, and technical meanings; analyze the impact of specific word choices on meaning and tone, including analogies or allusions to other texts.

Directions: Circle the best meaning for each underlined word.

1. The latest handheld devices incorporate <u>microprocessors</u>, which carry out complex functions rapidly and accurately.
   a. screens   b. computers   c. batteries   d. cases

2. A neutral nation sent diplomats to <u>mediate</u> between opposing forces in the ongoing conflict.
   a. rest   b. hurry   c. referee   d. stall

3. The year 2001 was the beginning of a new <u>millennium</u>.

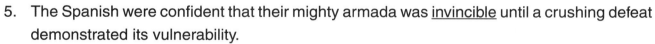

   a. thousand-year period   b. hundred-year period
   c. billion-year period   d. million-year period

4. An acid such as vinegar can <u>neutralize</u> a base such as baking soda.
   a. counteract   b. extend   c. strengthen   d. reinforce

5. The Spanish were confident that their mighty armada was <u>invincible</u> until a crushing defeat demonstrated its vulnerability.
   a. beautiful   b. sizable   c. unbeatable   d. unavoidable

6. The average <u>longevity</u> of Americans has improved from about 60 years in 1930 to almost 80 in 2010.
   a. height   b. weight   c. intelligence   d. lifespan

7. Scientists sometimes employ graduate students to <u>monitor</u> the progress of ongoing experiments.
   a. monetize   b. check   c. annihilate   d. publicize

8. The extinction of a species is usually considered irreversible, although the populations of many threatened species have <u>rebounded</u>.
   a. recovered   b. scrutinized   c. nosedived   d. plummeted

9. A poem by Emma Lazarus appears on the <u>pedestal</u> of the Statue of Liberty.
   a. torch   b. crown   c. base   d. gown

10. Ophthalmologists check <u>peripheral</u> vision as well as vision straight ahead.
   a. fringe   b. color   c. detail   d. photogenic

Challenge: Create a personal dictionary. Record unfamiliar words you encounter in science, history, and government texts, along with sample sentences and short definitions. Try to add at least one entry per day.

Name: _____   Date: _____

READING INFORMATIONAL TEXT: CRAFT AND STRUCTURE—
Analyzing a Paragraph

CCSS.ELA-LITERACY.RI.8.5: Analyze in detail the structure of a specific paragraph in a text, including the role of particular sentences in developing and refining a key concept.

Directions: Read the selection and answer the questions.

> The smallest unit of matter is called an atom. Just as letters are arranged in different ways to form all of the words in English, atoms combine to form all of the matter in the universe. There are 118 different kinds of atoms. Each atom has a center or nucleus. This nucleus contains at least one proton. Some nuclei also contain neutrons. A shell containing at least one electron usually surrounds the nucleus. For example, each atom in hydrogen, the most abundant element in the universe, has one proton in its nucleus and one electron in its shell. (A substance that contains only one kind of atom is called an *element*.) By contrast, the nucleus of a plutonium atom contains 94 protons and 150 neutrons. Atoms are the alphabet of everything.

1. Which sentence states the central idea? _____
   _____

2. What is the purpose of the second sentence? _____
   _____

3. Which technical terms are defined in this paragraph? _____
   _____

4. Which two elements are compared? _____
   a. What do they have in common? _____
      _____

   b. How do they differ? _____
      _____

5. Which sentence explains the relationship between atoms and elements? _____
   _____

6. Which sentence summarizes the paragraph? _____
   _____

Challenge: Choose a paragraph from a science or history text book.
On your own paper, explain the purpose of each sentence.
- Does the sentence state the central idea?
- Does it offer a comparison?
- Does it provide facts?
- Does it give an example?
- Does it summarize the paragraph?

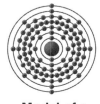

**Model of a
Plutonium Atom**

Name: _____   Date: _____

READING INFORMATIONAL TEXT: CRAFT AND STRUCTURE— Determining Purpose

CCSS.ELA-LITERACY.RI.8.6: Determine an author's point of view or purpose in a text and analyze how the author acknowledges and responds to conflicting evidence or viewpoints.

Directions: Read the selection and answer the questions.

Railroad Tracks Are Not a Shortcut

You may hear friends or relatives claim that it is perfectly safe to use railroad tracks as shortcuts or as trendy photographic backgrounds. They may point out how seldom trains roll by. They might even claim that strolling down the tracks is safer and more efficient than walking beside the road.

Don't listen. First, walking on railroad tracks is illegal. It is trespassing. Unlike roads or trails, railroad tracks are private property. More important, walking along the rails could cost you your life. This is not a myth or exaggeration. It is an indisputable fact. In the United States, approximately 500 people each year die as a direct result of walking along railroad tracks.

Certainly, most railroad tracks do not seem as busy as highways. Do not be deceived. Freight schedules are irregular. Some tracks are only used occasionally, but that does not mean the route has been abandoned. A train may roar through unexpectedly, day or night.

A railroad track is a dedicated right-of-way. On a public road, cars and trucks must stop for cross traffic. Trains, on their private tracks, do not stop. There is a good reason for that. Trains simply cannot stop as quickly as other vehicles. If a train is traveling at only 55 miles an hour, it takes more than a mile to come to a halt. Of course, many trains travel much faster than 55 miles an hour. The faster the train is traveling, the longer it takes to stop.

The next time someone tries to convince you to take a shortcut down the tracks, suggest a safer route.

1. What is the purpose of this selection? _____

_____

2. What opposing claims does the author present? _____

_____

_____

3. How does the author refute each claim? _____

_____

_____

4. What statistics does the author present? _____

_____

5. What ideas do the statistics support? _____

_____

Name: _____ Date: _____

READING INFORMATIONAL TEXT: INTEGRATION OF KNOWLEDGE AND IDEAS—When the Medium Looms Large

CCSS.ELA-LITERACY.RI.8.7: Evaluate the advantages and disadvantages of using different mediums (e.g., print or digital text, video, multimedia) to present a particular topic or idea.

Directions: On another paper, name the medium you would use to present each subject. Explain your choice.

> **a. typed report**   **b. blog**   **c. digital slideshow**   **d. video presentation**
> **e. podcast**   **f. other (explain)**

1. The structure of the atom
2. DNA and heredity
3. Phases of the moon
4. A book or film review
5. A restaurant review
6. A travel journal
7. A report about Beethoven's music
8. The causes of the Revolutionary War

9. Reconstruction after the Civil War
10. Positive and negative impacts of a new highway on a city
11. The impacts of the loss of top-level predators such as cougars or wolves on an ecosystem
12. A record of weather in a particular location over a period of three months
13. An explanation of the differences between chemical energy, thermal energy, mechanical energy, electrical energy, potential energy, and kinetic energy.
14. A report about marine food chains in the Arctic
15. A report about a great scientist and his most significant discoveries
16. A report about the history of the scientific method
17. A report about the effect of early automobiles on society
18. A report about folk music in the Appalachians
19. A report about the life of a famous author
20. A report about a famous artist and his or her work
21. A report about the lives of emancipated slaves after the Civil War
22. A report about the role of Chinese immigrants in the building of the transcontinental railroad
23. Publicity for school plays, athletic competitions, musical performances, and other public events
24. A talk for parents about how to help students succeed in school
25. An explanation of the circulatory system

Challenge: Read a text selection about a subject, such as marine life in the Arctic. View a video about the same subject. Then use a search engine to find a related blog. For example, the Ocean Conservancy offers "The Blog Aquatic" at <http://blog.oceanconservancy.org/tag/arctic-ocean/>. What are the advantages of each medium?

Name: _____   Date: _____

READING INFORMATIONAL TEXT: INTEGRATION OF KNOWLEDGE AND IDEAS—Evaluating the Author's Argument

CCSS.ELA-LITERACY.RI.8.8: Delineate and evaluate the argument and specific claims in a text, assessing whether the reasoning is sound and the evidence is relevant and sufficient; recognize when irrelevant evidence is introduced.

CCSS.ELA-LITERACY.RI.8.9: Analyze a case in which two or more texts provide conflicting information on the same topic and identify where the texts disagree on matters of fact or interpretation.

Directions: Read the following selections. Answer the questions on your own paper.

Advantages of Book Digitization

Digital books have many advantages. Thousands of volumes can be stored in a single handheld device. Because digital books are relatively inexpensive to produce and distribute, works about specialized topics can be published cost-effectively. Digitization has also made many out-of-print books available again.

Disadvantages of Book Digitization

There's nothing like the feel of a book printed on paper. An old-fashioned book can transport a reader to other times and places without electricity or Internet connections. Although travelers can carry thousands of books in a device, tablet and e-book batteries run down rapidly. Digital libraries are useless without power.

1. What argument does the writer offer in favor of book digitization? What other arguments could have been included?
2. What argument does the writer offer in favor of traditional books? What other arguments could have been included?
3. In your opinion, is a long-range compromise possible? If so, what is it? If not, why not?

Challenge: Analyzing Conflicting Information
Directions: Find two articles, one supporting each side of a controversial contemporary or historical issue. Which article is more convincing? Why? Write your answer on your own paper.
Suggested topics:
- Does intellectual ability depend on environmental factors more than genetics?
- Are low-fat foods healthy or unhealthy?
- Should the government ban sugary foods?
- Does freedom of speech protect bullies?
- Should all books be digitized?
- Should students be allowed to bring cell phones to school?
- Should the school day be shorter or longer?
- Should there be more or less homework?
- Is year-round school better than the traditional nine-month school year?

Name: _____   Date: _____

WRITING: TEXT TYPES AND PURPOSES, WRITE ARGUMENTS—Evidence Worksheet

CCSS.ELA-LITERACY.W.8.1: Write arguments to support claims with clear reasons and relevant evidence
CCSS.ELA-LITERACY.W.8.1.A: Introduce claim(s), acknowledge and distinguish the claim(s) from alternate or opposing claims, and organize the reasons and evidence logically.

Directions: Use this form to plan a persuasive essay. Choose a topic. Research arguments on both sides of the issue. Index cards are a good way to record information. Jot down reasons, examples, statistics, short quotations, and anecdotes on separate cards. Record the most convincing evidence here.

Claim: _____

Why the issue is important: _____

Opposing point of view: _____

Reason 1 for opposition: _____

Evidence: _____

Reason 2 for opposition: _____

Evidence: _____

Reason 1 for claim: _____

Evidence: _____

Reason 2 for claim: _____

Evidence: _____

Sample claims:
- Students should not have to take classes in subjects that do not interest them.
- Students should learn job skills in high school.
- All students should attend college.
- Everyone should study higher math.
- All students should study art, music, and drama.
- All students should volunteer in the community.
- Students should work for a year before starting college.
- Everyone should speak at least two languages.
- All landlords should allow pets.

Name: _____   Date: _____

WRITING: TEXT TYPES AND PURPOSES, WRITE ARGUMENTS—Review Planning Sheet

CCSS.ELA-LITERACY.W.8.1.B: Support claim(s) with logical reasoning and relevant evidence, using accurate, credible sources and demonstrating an understanding of the topic or text.
CCSS.ELA-LITERACY.W.8.1.C: Use words, phrases, and clauses to create cohesion and clarify the relationships among claim(s), counterclaims, reasons, and evidence.

Directions: Use the following form to plan a review. Include the most important ideas. Complete sentences are not necessary.

Title: _____

Reviewer: _____

Subject: _____

Type of review: (book, movie, music, video game, or restaurant) _____

Intended audience or customer: _____

Details: (examples: plot summary, cast/characters, special effects, or menu)

_____

_____

_____

_____

Background: (examples: author's previous works, plot or character sources, history of the specific type of food) _____

_____

_____

_____

Critical opinion: (examples: comparison to similar works, effectiveness)

_____

_____

_____

_____

Following the plan, write your final review on another paper. Include words and phrases such as the following to clarify the relationships between your ideas. Don't forget to start with an intriguing introduction and end with a conclusion that summarizes your ideas.

> **is similar to, is different from, differs from, although, instead, however, yet, similarly, while, on the one hand/on the other hand, likewise, whereas, consequently, for this reason, as a result of, if…then, this led to, therefore, in fact, for instance**

Name: _____   Date: _____

WRITING: TEXT TYPES AND PURPOSES, WRITE ARGUMENTS—Needed: A Constitution

CCSS.ELA-LITERACY.W.8.1.D: Establish and maintain a formal style.
CCSS.ELA-LITERACY.W.8.1.E: Provide a concluding statement or section that follows from and supports the argument presented.

Directions: Read the following arguments. On another paper, write an essay presenting them in your own words. Add a brief introduction and a concluding paragraph.

A. The Articles of Confederation were a compromise.

B. The Articles reserved most rights for the states.

C. Under the Articles of Confederation, the national government was responsible for defense and general welfare, but it was very weak.

D. The national government lacked many essential powers.

  1. Each state had one vote in Congress, which was not fair to the most populous states.

  2. Congress did not have the power to raise money through taxation.

  3. Each state printed its own money.

  4. States regulated imports and exports. Some states dealt directly with other nations.

  5. There was no court system or president, so there was no way to enforce national laws.

  6. Laws and amendments were almost impossible to pass.

    a. Laws needed nine votes out of 13 to pass.

    b. Amendments required a unanimous decision.

Challenge: Write a paragraph offering three reasons the Constitution was an improvement over the Articles of Confederation. Omit the conclusion. Exchange papers with a partner. Write a conclusion for your partner's essay.

Alternative topics:
  • Three ways the Enlightenment influenced America's revolutionary leaders.
  • Three reasons a national currency system was important.
  • Three reasons a national court system was important.
  • Three reasons the nation needed an easier way to pass laws and amendments.

WRITING: TEXT TYPES AND PURPOSES, WRITE INFORMATIVE/EXPLANATORY TEXTS—Brainstorming

CCSS.ELA-LITERACY.W.8.2: Write informative/explanatory texts to examine a topic and convey ideas, concepts, and information through the selection, organization, and analysis of relevant content.

CCSS.ELA-LITERACY.W.8.2.A: Introduce a topic clearly, previewing what is to follow; organize ideas, concepts, and information into broader categories; include formatting (e.g., headings), graphics (e.g., charts, tables), and multimedia when useful to aiding comprehension.

Directions: Choose a subject for a report. Use this organizer to jot down as many related ideas as possible before starting your research. Keep all of these elements in mind as you develop your paper. This is just a starting place. Feel free to add information or make adjustments as you work.

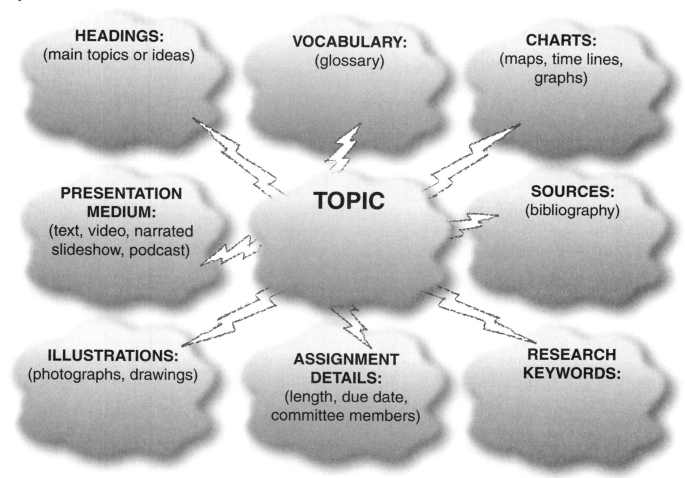

Sample topics:

The life of a famous American author
The Women's Suffrage Movement
Indentured servitude
Florence Nightingale
The nervous system, the skeletal system, or the muscular system

The life of an American President
Japanese Americans during World War II
The history of baseball, football, or basketball
Comets   Sunspots
Viruses

Name: _____   Date: _____

WRITING: TEXT TYPES AND PURPOSES, WRITE INFORMATIVE/EXPLANATORY TEXTS—Evidence Worksheet

CCSS.ELA-LITERACY.W.8.2.B: Develop the topic with relevant, well-chosen facts, definitions, concrete details, quotations, or other information and examples.

Directions: On another paper, write a short essay. Include at least one instance of each type of evidence. Use this worksheet to keep track of the evidence for your essay.

Topic: _____

Facts and Details: (complete sentences not necessary) _____

_____

_____

_____

Terms: _____   Definition: _____

_____   Definition: _____

_____   Definition: _____

_____   Definition: _____

Quotation: _____

Source: _____

Quotation: _____

Source: _____

Quotation: _____

Source: _____

Statistics: _____

_____

_____

Sample Topics:
- Reasons for the Monroe Doctrine
- The Invention of _____ (refrigeration, indoor plumbing, the pencil, etc.)
- The Impact of the California Gold Rush
- Yellow Journalism and the Spanish-American War
- An Introduction to the Mississippian Culture (Puebloan Culture, Inuit Culture, etc.)
- The Impact of _____ (the California Missions, the Interstate Highway System, etc.)
- The Importance of _____ (public libraries, public education, public parks, museums, orchestras, the postal service, the justice system, etc.)
- Requirements for Becoming a _____ (teacher, lawyer, healthcare worker, contractor, etc.)
- The Importance of Learning _____ (a second language, math, history, language arts, geography, civics, a trade, art, music, drama, etc.)

WRITING: TEXT TYPES AND PURPOSES, WRITE INFORMATIVE/EXPLANATORY TEXTS—Using Transitional Words and Phrases

CCSS.ELA-LITERACY.W.8.2.C: Use appropriate and varied transitions to create cohesion and clarify the relationships among ideas and concepts.

Directions: On another paper, write a paragraph using the following facts. Connect ideas and concepts with transitional words and phrases such as those listed in the box below.

> **initially, after, in spite of, following, during, in contrast to, preceding, due to, while, throughout, before, whenever, not only… but also, between, since, because, specifically, for instance, despite the fact that, as a result, therefore, thus, however, moreover, in conclusion, all things considered, nevertheless, in summary, to sum up, all in all, as a consequence, neither… nor, either… or, whether… or, first, second, third, last, on the one hand/on the other hand, although, even if, previous, all the same, subsequently, hence, for the duration of, finally**

1. Between 1846 and 1869, about 400,000 settlers traveled west in Conestoga wagons.
2. They journeyed from Independence, Missouri, to the Pacific Coast.
3. The trip took about five months.
4. The journey cost a family about $1,000.
5. Construction of the transcontinental railroad was begun in 1863, during the Civil War.
6. The Central Pacific Railroad Company built eastward from Sacramento.
7. The Union Pacific Railroad Company built westward from Council Bluffs, Iowa.
8. On May 10, 1869, the transcontinental railroad was completed.
9. In a famous ceremony, a golden spike joined the two lines.
10. It was driven at Promontory Summit in the Utah territory.
11. The new Pacific Railroad was 1,928 miles long.
12. It took one week to travel across the country.
13. The train fare for emigrants was $65.
14. Freight and passenger service was easier and less expensive.

Challenge: On your own paper, classify the words and phrases in the box above using the following categories:

Sequence; Cause/Effect; Comparison/Contrast; Item/Category; Summary

WRITING: TEXT TYPES AND PURPOSES, WRITE INFORMATIVE/EXPLANATORY TEXTS—Using Precise Vocabulary

CCSS.ELA-LITERACY.W.8.2.D: Use precise language and domain-specific vocabulary to inform about or explain the topic.
CCSS.ELA-LITERACY.W.8.2.E: Establish and maintain a formal style.

Directions: Use words from the box to complete the paragraph.

combatants	demolish	emancipation	acknowledge	perception
discord	galvanized	inhumane	quell	incompatible
resolve	undertake	rebellious	reconstruction	disgruntled
unify	preceding	opposition	seceded	

In the years 1) _____ the Civil War, 2) _____

was steadily increasing. The abolitionists in the north became more vocal in their

3) _____ to the 4) _____ practice of buying and

selling human beings. When Abraham Lincoln was elected in 1860, the South knew that he

would 5) _____ the task of phasing out slavery. The election

6) _____ forces in the South. One by one, 7) _____

states 8) _____ from the Union. 9) _____

confronted one another in battle after battle. On January 1, 1863, Lincoln signed the

10) _____ Proclamation, freeing the slaves. Then, in 1865, the South

surrendered. In the years after the war, the country struggled to 11) _____

itself again. This period is called the 12) _____ because it was a time

of rebuilding.

Challenge: Circle the words you did not use. Write a synonym for each.

_____

_____

_____

Name: _____   Date: _____

WRITING: TEXT TYPES AND PURPOSES, WRITE INFORMATIVE/EXPLANATORY TEXTS—Writing Conclusions

CCSS.ELA-LITERACY.W.8.2.F: Provide a concluding statement or section that follows from and supports the information or explanation presented.

Directions: Write a paragraph using all of the following facts. Include a title, an introductory sentence, and a conclusion. Use linking words and transitional phrases to connect the ideas.

- is the smallest building block of matter
- is invisible to the naked eye
- contains a nucleus
- the nucleus is in the center
- the nucleus always contains protons
- the nucleus usually contains neutrons
- electrons are in one or more shells around the nucleus

_____

_____

_____

_____

_____

_____

_____

_____

_____

_____

_____

_____

_____

_____

_____

_____

Challenge: On your own paper, write a paragraph about the characteristics of one of the following: comets, galaxies, ecosystems, cells, neurons, scientific method, acids, molecules, elements, cumulus clouds, or genes

Name: _____   Date: _____

WRITING: TEXT TYPES AND PURPOSES, WRITE NARRATIVES—Inspiration for Personal Narratives: Teacher Resource Page

> **CCSS.ELA-LITERACY.W.8.3:** Write narratives to develop real or imagined experiences or events using effective technique, relevant descriptive details, and well-structured event sequences.
> **CCSS.ELA-LITERACY.W.8.3.A:** Engage and orient the reader by establishing a context and point of view and introducing a narrator and/or characters; organize an event sequence that unfolds naturally and logically.

Suggest these ideas to your students for narrative writing assignments:

The Most Frightening Hour Ever

My Favorite Neighbor

My Worst Enemy

My Best Vacation

Graduation

Moving

We Won (or We Lost)

My Most Confusing Experience

My Biggest Mistake

And They Blamed Me

Too Late

The Most Important Thing I Ever Lost

The Person I Admire The Most

My Most Precious Possession

The Most Important Thing I Ever Learned

The First Person Who Admired Me

How I Met My Best Friend

My Worst Nightmare

The Worst Holiday Ever

Disaster

My First Day at Middle School

The Dentist (or The Doctor)

Envy (or Greed)

The Worst Dinner Ever

Lost

I Will Never Forget

They'll Never Understand

But I Didn't Give Up

My Proudest Moment

The Best Day of My Life

The Most Beautiful Place in the World

The Worst Road (or Field) Trip Ever

The Best Book I Ever Read (or The Best Movie I Ever Saw)

My First Car (train, plane, motorcycle, bus, horse, bicycle, or boat) Ride

Swimming (Dancing, Music, Gymnastics, or other) Lessons

Challenge: Encourage students to write a paragraph about a random word.

WRITING: TEXT TYPES AND PURPOSES, WRITE NARRATIVES—Using Narrative Techniques

CCSS.ELA-LITERACY.W.8.3.B: Use narrative techniques, such as dialogue, pacing, description, and reflection, to develop experiences, events, and/or characters.

1. Write a description of a school. Include evocative sensory details such as smells, sounds, temperature, and, of course, specific visual information.

_____

_____

_____

_____

_____

2. Write a dialogue between two students about an upcoming school event.

_____

_____

_____

_____

_____

_____

3. Write a paragraph in which a character wonders what another character is thinking.

_____

_____

_____

_____

_____

4. On your own paper, use your responses to the prompts above to write a short story. Feel free to change the names and details, but be sure to include dialogue, description, and interior monologue in your finished work.

Challenge: On another paper, use dialogue, description, and interior monologue to relate a memorable event from your own experience. Select an episode with a natural beginning, middle, and end.

Name: _____   Date: _____

WRITING: TEXT TYPES AND PURPOSES, WRITE NARRATIVES—Orienting the Reader With Transition Words

CCSS.ELA-LITERACY.W.8.3.C: Use a variety of transition words, phrases, and clauses to convey sequence, signal shifts from one time frame or setting to another, and show the relationships among experiences and events.

Directions: Write the best transition word on each line. Finish the story using words and phrases from the box.

> **before, after, while, during, between, near, beyond, about _____ miles from, approximately, following, preceding, initially, at first, later, when, then, since, as a result, consequently, throughout, amid, amongst, all through, subsequently, past, whereas**

1. Even _____ Sam left the house that morning, he had a sense of impending doom.

2. The feeling intensified _____ his walk through the neighborhood.

3. _____ the intersection at Elm and Mason and the west gate of the campus, the trees seemed to be reaching for him.

4. _____, he dismissed his fear as irrational.

5. However, _____ that afternoon, he realized he should have paid attention to his intuition.

_____

_____

_____

_____

_____

_____

_____

_____

_____

Challenge: Print out the first page of a public domain short story, then circle all of the transitional words and phrases. Notice how the author uses these signals to connect his or her ideas.

WRITING: TEXT TYPES AND PURPOSES, WRITE NARRATIVES—Employing Precise Vocabulary

CCSS.ELA-LITERACY.W.8.3.D: Use precise words and phrases, relevant descriptive details, and sensory language to capture the action and convey experiences and events.

Directions: Write the best descriptive term from the box on each line. Synonyms are provided as clues. Complete the story. Continue on the back of this page or your own paper if necessary.

ornate	agile	articulate	avid	balmy	bizarre
blasé	gaunt	preposterous	gingerly	sublime	ungainly

The Visitor

The summer night was 1) _____ (pleasant) with a gentle breeze

from the south. A 2) _____, (thin) 3) _____ (clumsy)

figure crossed the parking lot, stepping 4) _____ (cautiously) over a

patch of recently watered lawn. When the visitor reached the auditorium, a

5) _____ (bored) student in a 6) _____ (ridiculous)

red usher's jacket sprang into action and opened the door for him. Several

7) _____ (enthusiastic) fans accompanied him down the aisle to the stage.

Everyone knew the renowned author would be charming and 8) _____

(well spoken), but nobody was prepared for the 9) _____ (transcendent)

new work he presented.

_____

_____

_____

_____

Challenge: On another paper, write a short story using as many of the following words as possible.

unsettling	urban	vacant	vague	sinister	significant
reckless	plight	postpone	self-assured	levitate	improbably
semicircle					

WRITING: TEXT TYPES AND PURPOSES, WRITE NARRATIVES—Endings

CCSS.ELA-LITERACY.W.8.3.E: Provide a conclusion that follows from and reflects on the narrated experiences or events.

Directions: Write conclusions for these story ideas. The endings can be funny, frightening, happy, or sad, but they should fit the situations.

1. Mrs. Mills, a temperamental widow, fires her maid because she suspects the longtime servant of theft. Later that evening, Mrs. Mills finds the missing item in a drawer.

    _____

    _____

    _____

    _____

2. Mr. Samuels loves to collect junk. One day he brings home a particularly hideous monstrosity. When his wife complains, he tries to get rid of it, but it keeps reappearing in the house.

    _____

    _____

    _____

    _____

3. Mike, David's little brother, is impulsive. He's always doing foolish things. One afternoon, when their mother is out interviewing for a new job, Mike climbs a tree in the front yard and falls.

    _____

    _____

    _____

    _____

4. The city has announced the scheduled demolition of a ramshackle apartment house on Tom's street. Tom is aware that an elderly couple has been living there. He knows they will have nowhere to go. Tom and some friends start a campaign to find them a new home before the wrecking crew arrives.

    _____

    _____

    _____

    _____

Challenge: Discuss your ideas with a partner. Then, on another paper, develop one of the plots into a short story. Include description, dialogue, interior monologue, and intriguing complications.

WRITING: PRODUCTION AND DISTRIBUTION OF WRITING—First Draft Critique

CCSS.ELA-LITERACY.W.8.4: Produce clear and coherent writing in which the development, organization, and style are appropriate to task, purpose, and audience. (Grade-specific expectations for writing types are defined in Standards 1-3 above.)

CCSS.ELA-LITERACY.W.8.5: With some guidance and support from peers and adults, develop and strengthen writing as needed by planning, revising, editing, rewriting, or trying a new approach, focusing on how well purpose and audience have been addressed. (Editing for conventions should demonstrate command of Language Standards 1-3 up to and including Grade 8 here.)

Directions: Fill out this suggestion page for a partner's short story or essay. Make any needed corrections on a copy of the draft with a red or blue pen.

Title: _____

Author: _____   Editor: _____

What is the purpose of this story or article? _____

_____

Underline any sentences that do not fit the purpose.

What else would you like to know about the setting? _____

_____

Does the author use sentence variety? _____

Does the author use transitional words and phrases? _____ If not, use question marks to denote places where transitions would make the text easier to understand.

Circle any words that are spelled incorrectly. Correct any punctuation or capitalization errors.

Is the dialogue natural? _____ If not, how could it be improved? _____

_____

_____

What is each character's problem? _____

_____

_____

_____

Does the conclusion fit this story or essay? _____ Why or why not? _____

_____

_____

Additional comments or suggestions: _____

_____

_____

Name: _____ Date: _____

WRITING: PRODUCTION AND DISTRIBUTION OF WRITING—Technology Resources: Teacher Resource Page

CCSS.ELA-LITERACY.W.8.6: Use technology, including the Internet, to produce and publish writing and present the relationships between information and ideas efficiently as well as to interact and collaborate with others.

Internet Resources:
Public domain photo sources: American Memory: http://memory.loc.gov/
NASA Education: http://www.nasa.gov/audience/forstudents/
Public Domain Sherpa: http://www.publicdomainsherpa.com/public-domain-photographs.html
U.S. Government Photos and Images: http://www.usa.gov/Topics/Graphics.shtml
Wikimedia Commons: http://commons.wikimedia.org/wiki/Main_Page
Public domain music sources: Public Domain 4u: http://publicdomain4u.com/
Musopen: https://musopen.org/
Partners in Rhyme Sound Effects: http://www.partnersinrhyme.com/pir/PIRsfx.shtml
Chart-making tools: Create a Graph: http://nces.ed.gov/nceskids/createagraph/
Top 10 Free Timeline Creation Tools for Teachers: http://elearningindustry.com/top-10-free-timeline-creation-tools-for-teachers
Outline Map Sites: http://www.lib.utexas.edu/maps/map_sites/outline_sites.html
Web 2.0: Cool Tools for Schools: http://cooltoolsforschools.wikispaces.com/Organiser+Tools
Grammar and usage resources: University of Chicago Writing Program Grammar Resources: http://writing-program.uchicago.edu/resources/grammar.htm
Purdue Online Writing Lab (OWL): https://owl.english.purdue.edu/owl/
"Top 10 Websites for Teaching Grammar To Your Students": http://edtechreview.in/e-learning/1187-top-10-websites-for-teaching-your-students-grammar
Spelling resources: "NEA: Spelling and Vocabulary, Grades 6-8": http://www.nea.org/tools/lessons/spelling-and-vocabulary-6-8.html
Presentation resources: "10 Presentation Tools for Students": http://www.avatargeneration.com/2012/07/10-presentation-tools-for-students/
Collaboration resources: "The Top 27 Free Tools to Collaborate, Hold Discussions, and Backchannel with Students," *Educational Technology and Mobile Learning:* http://www.educatorstechnology.com/2012/08/the-top-27-free-tools-to-collaborate.html
Online Quiz Makers: Quiz Star: http://quizstar.4teachers.org/
"Game and Puzzle Makers," *Internet4Classrooms:* http://www.internet4classrooms.com/links_grades_kindergarten_12/game_puzzle_makers_teacher_tools.htm
Project Ideas:
Podcasts of original short stories   Fan fiction for novels studied in class
Electronic presentations of poetry readings, illustrated with student art or photography
Videotaped presentations of short original plays or skits
Readers Theater using the best student short stories
Weekly blogs on the school website (approve the text before posting)
Letter exchanges with classes in other parts of the country, describing field trips and other school experiences
Skype visits with authors or people who live in locales featured in stories or poems.

Name: _____ Date: _____

WRITING: RESEARCH TO BUILD AND PRESENT KNOWLEDGE—Writing a Research Paper

CCSS.ELA-LITERACY.W.8.7: Conduct short research projects to answer a question (including a self-generated question), drawing on several sources and generating additional related, focused questions that allow for multiple avenues of exploration.
CCSS.ELA-LITERACY.W.8.8: Gather relevant information from multiple print and digital sources, using search terms effectively; assess the credibility and accuracy of each source; and quote or paraphrase the data and conclusions of others while avoiding plagiarism and following a standard format for citation.
CCSS.ELA-LITERACY.W.8.9: Draw evidence from literary or informational texts to support analysis, reflection, and research.

Directions: Write a short research paper to answer one of the following questions.

1. What were the causes of the American Revolution?
2. What were the causes of the American Civil War?
3. How did the transcontinental railroad change the United States?
4. How did the interstate highway system change the United States?
5. When and where were the major gold and silver rushes in the United States? What effect did each of them have on the nation?
6. What effect did the development of steamships have on the United States?
7. Why was Henry Ford able to sell cars more inexpensively than other early carmakers? What effect did this have on the country?
8. What was the Pony Express? How did it operate? Why did it last only a short time?
9. What happened to freed slaves after the Civil War? What problems did they face? How did they overcome those problems?
10. What is the balance of power in the federal government? Find a current example of how it is working or why it is now controversial.
11. How and why have Eastern forests changed since the arrival of the Europeans?
12. How and why has the Central Plains ecosystem changed since the arrival of the Europeans?
13. How did the arrival of the Spanish in Mexico change the lives of indigenous peoples in what is now the Midwestern United States?
14. What was The Long Walk? Why did it take place? How did it change the lives and cultures of the people involved?
15. Who are the Puebloans? Where do they live now? Who were their ancestors?
16. What is jazz? Where did it began? Who were some famous practitioners? What influence has it had?
17. What was the center for whaling in the United States? What were some important products derived from whales? What influence did whaling have on American culture? Does whaling still take place? If so, where and why?
18. In what ways did the peace treaty that ended World War I sow the seeds for World War II?

Name: _____   Date: _____

WRITING: RESEARCH TO BUILD AND PRESENT KNOWLEDGE/ RANGE OF WRITING—Keeping Journals

CCSS.ELA-LITERACY.W.8.9.A: Apply Grade 8 Reading Standards to literature (e.g., "Analyze how a modern work of fiction draws on themes, patterns of events, or character types from myths, traditional stories, or religious works such as the Bible, including describing how the material is rendered new.").

CCSS.ELA-LITERACY.W.8.9.B: Apply Grade 8 Reading Standards to literary nonfiction (e.g., "Delineate and evaluate the argument and specific claims in a text, assessing whether the reasoning is sound and the evidence is relevant and sufficient; recognize when irrelevant evidence is introduced.").

CCSS.ELA-LITERACY.W.8.10: Write routinely over extended time frames (time for research, reflection, and revision) and shorter time frames (a single sitting or a day or two) for a range of discipline-specific tasks, purposes, and audiences.

Reading Journal

Directions: In a dedicated notebook, jot down the following information for each book you read. Keep your notes for reference.

Fiction
Title:
Author:
Hero (Protagonist):
Villain (Antagonist):
Hero's Allies:
Villain's Allies:
Hero's Main Problem (goal):
Obstacles to Accomplishing the Goal:
Villain's Main Problem (goal):
Obstacles to Accomplishing the Goal:
Theme:
Setting: (time); (place)
Similarities to a Traditional Character
   or Story:

Nonfiction
Title:
Author:
Subject:
Author's Purpose:
   (inform, persuade, or entertain)
Central Idea 1:
Type of Proof
   (facts, quotations, anecdotes, etc.)
Central Idea 2:
Type of Proof
   (facts, quotations, anecdotes, etc.)
Central Idea 3:
Type of Proof
   (facts, quotations, anecdotes, etc.)
Effectiveness:
   (Does this work achieve its purpose?)

Writing Journal

Directions: Write an entry in a dedicated notebook each day. Here are some suggestions.

short short fiction or poetry (50–100 words); special school events; unusual weather; sports; facts and observations regarding interesting people you have met, seen in the media, or read about; reviews of books, music, cafés, shops, movies, or plays; accounts of personal experiences such as trips, competitions, embarrassing situations, or disappointments; extracurricular projects

Name: _____   Date: _____

SPEAKING AND LISTENING: COMPREHENSION AND COLLABORATION—Discussion Record Sheet

CCSS.ELA-LITERACY.SL.8.1: Engage effectively in a range of collaborative discussions (one-on-one, in groups, and teacher-led) with diverse partners on Grade 8 topics, texts, and issues, building on others' ideas and expressing their own clearly.
CCSS.ELA-LITERACY.SL.8.1.A: Come to discussions prepared, having read or researched material under study; explicitly draw on that preparation by referring to evidence on the topic, text, or issue to probe and reflect on ideas under discussion.

Directions: Complete this information for each discussion. Notice how your skills improve with practice.

Discussion Date: _____

Participants: (Circle One)   Class   Partner   Small Group   Other

Subject: _____

Sources you consulted: (Circle one or more)   Article   Textbook Chapter   Internet
          Novel   Newspaper   Book   Other

List titles and authors: _____

_____

_____

Discussion Question: _____

_____

Point 1: _____

Best Evidence: _____

Point 2: _____

Best Evidence: _____

Point 3: _____

Best Evidence: _____

Vocabulary: _____

_____

Notes: _____

_____

Evaluation

I learned: _____

I wish I had read more about: _____

I am interested in finding out more about: _____

This discussion would have been even better if _____

_____

Name: _____   Date: _____

SPEAKING AND LISTENING: COMPREHENSION AND COLLABORATION—Committee Planning Sheet

CCSS.ELA-LITERACY.SL.8.1.B: Follow rules for collegial discussions and decision-making, track progress toward specific goals and deadlines, and define individual roles as needed.

Directions: Use this planning sheet for your committee meetings.

COMMITTEE MEMBERS

Chairperson: _____

Recorder: _____

Other: _____

Other: _____

AGENDAS

Meeting 1: Planning

Meeting 2: Progress

Meeting 3. Fulfillment

Meeting 4: Evaluation

GOAL

_____
_____

RULES

- _____
  _____
- _____
  _____
- _____
  _____
- _____
  _____

(Establish these at the first meeting.)

DECISIONS

- _____
  _____
- _____
  _____
- _____
  _____
- _____
  _____

Name: _____   Date: _____

SPEAKING AND LISTENING: COMPREHENSION AND COLLABORATION—Discussion Worksheet

CCSS.ELA-LITERACY.SL.8.1.C: Pose questions that connect the ideas of several speakers and respond to others' questions and comments with relevant evidence, observations, and ideas.

CCSS.ELA-LITERACY.SL.8.1.D: Acknowledge new information expressed by others, and, when warranted, qualify or justify their own views in light of the evidence presented.

Directions: Use this sheet to take notes during a discussion.

Subject: _____   Date: _____

Circle one: class discussion   partner discussion   small-group discussion

Speaker #1: _____

Speaker's Idea or question: _____

My idea, question, or response: _____

_____

Speaker #2: _____

Speaker's Idea or question: _____

My idea, question, or response: _____

_____

Evaluation

My ideas about this subject before the discussion: _____

_____

_____

_____

Three ways the discussion affected my thinking about this topic:

1. _____

2. _____

3. _____

Challenge: Record or videotape a small-group discussion. As a group, review the recording. Notice: 1. Did the participants stay on topic? 2. Did they accurately summarize points made by others before responding? 3. Did they add new information to defend their positions, if necessary? 4. Did they share evidence such as examples, statistics, relevant personal experiences, or quotations from experts? 5. Did all participants share in the conversation, or did one person dominate? 6. Was everyone prepared? If not, how did this affect the discussion?

SPEAKING AND LISTENING: COMPREHENSION AND COLLABORATION—Evidence, Fallacies, and Taking Notes: Teacher Resource Page

CCSS.ELA-LITERACY.SL.8.2: Analyze the purpose of information presented in diverse media and formats (e.g., visually, quantitatively, orally) and evaluate the motives (e.g., social, commercial, political) behind its presentation.

CCSS.ELA-LITERACY.SL.8.3: Delineate a speaker's argument and specific claims, evaluating the soundness of the reasoning and relevance and sufficiency of the evidence and identifying when irrelevant evidence is introduced.

Suggested Media to Evaluate for Purpose, Relevance, and Sufficient Evidence

News: gossip, local and national newspapers, news websites, television and radio news

Advertising: magazines, newspapers, television, Internet, billboards, radio, junk mail

Political campaigns: school election speeches, newspapers, town hall debates, television advertising, mailers, Internet sites

Books – Issues: energy, water, climate, education, wages, poverty, transportation, healthcare

Speakers: guest speakers at school, visiting authors, Ted talks, broadcasts of political speeches, sales pitches, famous speeches archived online

Kinds of Support or Evidence: statistics, quotations from experts, examples, anecdotes

Selected Logical Fallacies: (Caution students to avoid using these arguments in discussions or essays. There are many more than those listed below. To explore them, see <https://owl. english. perdue. edu/owl/resource 659/03/> or do a keyword search for *logical fallacies*.)

Straw man: Oversimplify your opponent's view. Then attack your oversimplification in your argument.

Slippery slope: If one thing happens, inevitably a chain of events will follow (usually extreme.)

Hasty generalization: Drawing broad conclusions from a few instances. Example: My sister never studies and has an excellent grade average. Therefore, studying is unnecessary.

Faulty cause and effect: If one thing happened, and something else happened after that, the first event caused the second.

Origin fallacy: Assert that the origin of an idea or person determines the value of that idea or person.

Ad hominem: Attack an opponent personally rather than addressing the issue.

Hints for taking effective notes:

- Write important words only.
- Write main ideas.
- Write important statistics.
- Write questions for further investigation.
- Use underlining to emphasize important points.
- Write keywords.
- Write names of cited experts.

Name: _____ Date: _____

SPEAKING AND LISTENING: PRESENTATION OF KNOWLEDGE AND IDEAS—Convince Us

> **CCSS.ELA-LITERACY.SL.8.4:** Present claims and findings, emphasizing salient points in a focused, coherent manner with relevant evidence; sound, valid reasoning; and well-chosen details; use appropriate eye contact, adequate volume, and clear pronunciation.
> **CCSS.ELA-LITERACY.SL.8.5:** Integrate multimedia and visual displays into presentations to clarify information, strengthen claims and evidence, and add interest.
> **CCSS.ELA-LITERACY.SL.8.6:** Adapt speech to a variety of contexts and tasks, demonstrating command of formal English when indicated or appropriate. (See Grade 8 Language Standards 1 and 3 here for specific expectations.)

Directions: Create a convincing presentation about one of the topics in the box.

> **Should Schools Have Dress Codes? Is Summer Vacation Important or Just Lost Learning Time? Should Schools Require Parenting Classes for Teens? Do Animals Have Rights? Should Schools Assign More or Less Homework? Is Feminism Important? Are There Any Limits on Free Speech? Should Schools Teach Cursive Writing? Should Schools Teach Trades in Middle School and High School? Is College Necessary? Are Cities More Efficient Than Suburbs? Standing Up Against Bullying: Is It a Good Idea? Should More People Work or Study From Home? Sports Safety Equipment: Should There Be More Laws?**

Planning Sheet

Major Point 1: _____

_____

Major Point 2: _____

_____

Major Point 3: _____

_____

Media/Equipment: (Circle the presentation aids you plan to use. Notify the teacher in advance so the necessary equipment will be available.)

    computer   projector   photographs   video clips   recordings

    charts and graphs   handouts

Practice Evaluation: (Rate your partner's practice presentation. Fifty is a perfect score.)

Eye contact:	1	2	3	4	5	6	7	8	9	10
Volume:	1	2	3	4	5	6	7	8	9	10
Enunciation:	1	2	3	4	5	6	7	8	9	10
Coherence:	1	2	3	4	5	6	7	8	9	10
Persuasiveness:	1	2	3	4	5	6	7	8	9	10

Name: _____ Date: _____

LANGUAGE: CONVENTIONS OF STANDARD ENGLISH— Understanding Verbals

CCSS.ELA-LITERACY.L.8.1: Demonstrate command of the conventions of standard English grammar and usage when writing or speaking.
CCSS.ELA-LITERACY.L.8.1.A: Explain the function of verbals (gerunds, participles, infinitives) in general and their function in particular sentences.

Directions: Read and follow the instructions for each item.

1. Underline the ***gerund*** or ***gerund phrase***. Circle its function in the sentence.
   a. Walking to school afforded Sean a modicum of independence.
      adjective   subject   direct object   object of preposition
   b. Sean hated walking to school.
      adjective   subject   direct object   object of preposition
   c. Because Mister Carson offered him a ride, Sean had a break from walking to school.
      adjective   subject   direct object   object of preposition

2. Underline the ***present participle***. Circle its function in the sentence.
   a. The birds were singing so loudly that they woke Mike up.   adjective   verb tense
   b. The birds had been singing, but they stopped.   adjective   verb tense
   c. The singing birds awoke Mike before dawn.   adjective   verb tense

3. Underline the ***past participle***. Circle its function in the sentence.
   a. The meaning was implied by her tone of voice.   adjective   verb tense
   b. The implied meaning of her remark was annoying.   adjective   verb tense
   c. The meaning will be implied by the context.   adjective   verb tense

4. Underline the ***infinitive***. Circle its function in the sentence.
   a. Magellan attempted to circumnavigate the globe.
      subject   object   modifier
   b. She brought a sandwich to eat in case the restaurants at the beach were too expensive.
      subject   object   modifier
   c. To err is human.
      subject   object   modifier

Challenge: On your own paper, write the gerund, past participle, and infinitive forms of each verb in the box.

> invigorate, galvanize, dramatize, facilitate, illuminate, envelop, glorify, deflate, unify

LANGUAGE: CONVENTIONS OF STANDARD ENGLISH— Using the Active and the Passive Voice

CCSS.ELA-LITERACY.L.8.1.B: Form and use verbs in the active and passive voice.

Directions: Read and follow the instructions for each item.

1. Write the passive form of each verb, and then use it in a sentence.

   a. illuminates   is _____ by

   _____

   b. implies   is _____ by

   _____

   c. neutralizes   is _____ by

   _____

   d. absorbs   is _____ by

   _____

   e. mandates   is _____ by

   _____

   f. initials   is _____ by

   _____

   g. electrifies   is _____ by

2. Write the active form of each passive verb phrase.

   a. is cited by   _____

   b. is compelled by   _____

   c. is deflated by   _____

   d. is deleted by   _____

   e. is designated by   _____

3. On another page, rewrite each passive sentence using an active verb form.
   a. Those files were deleted by the office manager.
   b. The examination questions were accidentally disclosed by the instructor's son.
   c. The last historic hotel downtown was demolished by a developer.
   d. The events following the earthquake were chronicled by a teenager living near the epicenter.
   e. The entire valley was enveloped in a dense cloud of noxious fumes.
   f. That particular film was banned by a local group last year, but it is available now.
   g. The country was unified by a newly elected leader.

LANGUAGE: CONVENTIONS OF STANDARD ENGLISH— What's a Mood?

CCSS.ELA-LITERACY.L.8.1.C: Form and use verbs in the indicative, imperative, interrogative, conditional, and subjunctive mood.
CCSS.ELA-LITERACY.L.8.1.D: Recognize and correct inappropriate shifts in verb voice and mood.*

Indicative: makes a statement   **Imperative:** expresses a command
Interrogative: asks a question   **Conditional:** used with *if, unless,* or *when*
Subjunctive: a wish or doubt

Directions: Read and follow the instructions for each section.

1. Circle the best verb form for each sentence.

    a. _____ that situation quickly or someone from the administration will be forced to step in.

    > resolved   resolve   resolving

    b. Who _____ Abraham Lincoln in the play tomorrow night?

    > portrayed   will portray   was portraying

    c. The mayor _____ dissent by listening to representatives from both sides of the issue.

    > quell   quelled   quelling

    d. If I were in charge of this committee, I _____ this differently.

    > will handle   would handle   have handled

    e. Sometimes, the general wished he _____ his superior's offer to retire.

    > will accept   had accepted   would accept

2. On your own paper, rewrite each sentence, correcting the verb forms.
    a. If the ambassador was as high-minded as he pretended to be, he <u>will have</u> extended his hospitality to all of the visiting dignitaries.
    b. The rogue soldier doubted that his siblings <u>joined</u> him in the coming fight.
    c. I wish my friends <u>will vote</u> for me in the upcoming school elections.
    d. If I was less self-conscious, I am certain I <u>will be</u> more successful.
    e. The entrepreneur wished he <u>can overcome</u> the perception that he was greedy.

Challenge: Identify the mood of the verb in each of the sentences in Section 1.

Name: _____ Date: _____

LANGUAGE: CONVENTIONS OF STANDARD ENGLISH— Using the Comma, Ellipsis, and Dash

CCSS.ELA-LITERACY.L.8.2: Demonstrate command of the conventions of standard English capitalization, punctuation, and spelling when writing.
CCSS.ELA-LITERACY.L.8.2.A: Use punctuation (comma, ellipsis, dash) to indicate a pause or break.

Directions: Place the indicated punctuation mark in each sentence to clarify the meaning or increase dramatic effect.

1. (comma) Of course the issue of slavery was an important factor in the Civil War.

2. (2 dashes) The plains not the mountains were Sarah's true home.

3. (ellipsis) The damage wasn't irreversible just serious.

4. (2 dashes) The excerpt as incriminating as it was could not be trusted outside of its context.

5. (2 dashes) The old man said, "I hoped no I dreamed you would return."

6. (comma) In fact Kara was an exceptional performer.

7. (ellipsis) "I never thought that" Abbey's voice trailed off.

8. (2 dashes) The lake undisturbed by a single ripple was an especially serene sight.

9. (comma) Mrs. Johnson are you planning to attend our meeting?

10. (ellipsis) Stacy ran until his legs turned to rubber and then he ran some more.

11. (two commas) Jason's younger brother though usually gullible saw through the scheme.

12. (2 dashes) Terry's current obsession cleaning up the beach was consuming all of her free time.

13. Write a line of character dialogue using an ellipsis. _____
_____

14. Write a sentence using two dashes. _____
_____

15. Write a sentence using two commas to set off parenthetical information. _____
_____
_____

16. Write a sentence using a comma to set off an introductory word or phrase. _____
_____
_____

Challenge: Find a sentence using a dash, an ellipsis, or a comma in a novel, short story, or article. Copy the sentence without punctuation. Challenge a partner to punctuate it correctly.

Name: _____ Date: _____

LANGUAGE: CONVENTIONS OF STANDARD ENGLISH—
Using an Ellipsis in a Quotation

CCSS.ELA-LITERACY.L.8.2.B: Use an ellipsis to indicate an omission.

Directions: Read and follow the instructions for each section.

1. Rewrite each sentence as a quotation. Replace an unneeded phrase with an ellipsis. Do not change the meaning of the sentence.

   a. The eccentric old man dressed in a shabby suit and worn-out shoes was actually a respected member of the city's elite.

   _____

   _____

   b. Members of the senior class will be there in spite of their other obligations to facilitate accurate record-keeping.

   _____

   _____

   c. In an effort to woo readers, some newspaper articles portray disasters in painful, tedious, deplorable, over-vivid, horrendous detail.

   _____

   _____

   d. A lunar eclipse, an astonishingly beautiful phenomenon, is easier to view than a solar eclipse.

   _____

   _____

2. Find three long, complex sentences in a story or text. Quote them here. Omit a section in each one. Retain the meaning of each sentence. Use ellipses to signal the omissions.

   a. _____

   _____

   b. _____

   _____

   c. _____

   _____

Challenge: Find a book or film advertisement that uses ellipses to quote parts of a review. Then read the full review. Was the meaning changed? In your opinion, is this honest? Why or why not?

Name: _____ Date: _____

LANGUAGE: CONVENTIONS OF STANDARD ENGLISH— Spelling

CCSS.ELA-LITERACY.L.8.2.C: Spell correctly.

Part 1: Circle the misspelled word in each sentence. Write the correct spelling.

1. The statue's pedistle was cracked. _____

2. The speaker was impressive and selfussured. _____

3. We didn't enjoy the sequal as much as the original novel. _____

4. My sister's stationary is embossed with her initials. _____

5. El Niño conditions recurr every few years. _____

6. Fear of the spreading epidemic escalated to histeria. _____

7. The dessert was topped with luschus strawberries. _____

8. The actress was talented but far too vane to achieve lasting success. _____

9. The workshop leader arrived to fascilitate a discussion. _____

10. One of the sinks in the second-floor lavaritory was broken. _____

11. We are now living in the third milennium. _____

12. Victims had to wait for emergency workers to clear the ubstruction. _____

Part 2: Circle the word that is spelled incorrectly.

13.	rational	renown	porus	amiss
14.	advokate	embark	onslaught	ovation
15.	proficient	adjile	rebuke	recourse
16.	revenue	audacious	inhance	ardent
17.	pungent	asimmilate	preposterous	rankle
18.	awry	fallacy	atrocity	avud
19.	trepudation	swelter	turbulent	deface
20.	irascible	surpass	sporatic	decipher

Challenge: Keep a private page in your notebook to record the correct spellings of words you have misspelled in assignments. The spell-checker in your word-processing program is amazing, but some misspellings are real words, just not the real words you wanted to use. Always have someone else read your paper before you turn it in.

Name: _____ Date: _____

LANGUAGE: KNOWLEDGE OF LANGUAGE—Creating Effects With Voice and Mood

CCSS.ELA-LITERACY.L.8.3: Use knowledge of language and its conventions when writing, speaking, reading, or listening.
CCSS.ELA-LITERACY.L.8.3.A: Use verbs in the active and passive voice and in the conditional and subjunctive mood to achieve particular effects (e.g., emphasizing the actor or the action; expressing uncertainty or describing a state contrary to fact).

Part 1: Write the phrase that best describes the effect of each sentence on the line provided.

> **emphasizes the actor** **emphasizes the action**
> **expresses uncertainty** **describes a state contrary to fact**

1. If our team wins today, it will be because of David and Stephen.

   _____

2. Our team was led to victory through the efforts of David and Stephen.

   _____

3. I wish our team had won the championship and not just today's game.

   _____

4. David and Stephen overhauled our offensive strategy and led the team to victory.

   _____

Part 2: Write a sentence that matches each instruction.

5. Write a sentence that emphasizes the actor. (Use the active voice.)

   _____

   _____

6. Write a sentence that emphasizes the action. (Use the passive voice.)

   _____

   _____

7. Write a sentence that expresses uncertainty. (Use a word like *if*.)

   _____

   _____

8. Write a sentence that expresses a condition contrary to fact. (Use a word like *wish*.)

   _____

   _____

Name: _____ Date: _____

LANGUAGE: VOCABULARY ACQUISITION AND USE—
Expanding Your Vocabulary

CCSS.ELA-LITERACY.L.8.4: Determine or clarify the meaning of unknown and multiple-meaning words or phrases based on Grade 8 reading and content, choosing flexibly from a range of strategies.

CCSS.ELA-LITERACY.L.8.4.A: Use context (e.g., the overall meaning of a sentence or paragraph; a word's position or function in a sentence) as a clue to the meaning of a word or phrase.

Directions: Define each underlined word.

1. Unfortunately, many wounded soldiers <u>succumbed</u> to infections before the invention of antibiotics.

   _____

2. Customs officers were able to <u>confiscate</u> the stolen paintings at the airport.

   _____

3. For years, the author allowed his talent to <u>languish</u> before he finally gathered the courage to complete his novel and send it to a publisher.

   _____

4. That crime falls under federal, not state <u>jurisdiction</u>.

   _____

5. The praying mantis is a <u>voracious</u> predator.

   _____

6. Everyone knew Carlos' uncle was an <u>irascible</u> old coot, but they also suspected that beneath his prickly exterior lurked a tender heart.

   _____

7. Sometimes Wiley's heavy frontier <u>dialect</u> could be difficult for his new New York neighbors to understand.

   _____

8. Daniel was confined to an isolation ward because the virus was extremely <u>contagious</u>.

   _____

9. Joshua called Kaylee his <u>muse</u> because he did better paintings when she was around.

   _____

10. Pete's friends attempted to <u>intervene</u>, but it was too late to help him.

   _____

Challenge: On your own paper, write a paragraph using at least five of the words you defined on this page.

Name: _____   Date: _____

LANGUAGE: VOCABULARY ACQUISITION AND USE—
Speaking of Latin and Greek (Roots That Is)

CCSS.ELA-LITERACY.L.8.4.B: Use common, grade-appropriate Greek or Latin affixes and roots as clues to the meaning of a word (e.g., *precede, recede, secede*).

Directions: Circle the meaning of each underlined Greek or Latin root.

1. <u>auto</u>nomy:	car	self	machine
2. <u>ann</u>als:	year	magazine	month
3. <u>biblio</u>graphy:	writing	list	book
4. em<u>brace</u>:	hug	arm	love
5. de<u>capit</u>ate:	execute	take	head
6. <u>cent</u>imeter:	hundred	measure	inch
7. <u>corpor</u>ation:	body	business	company
8. <u>deci</u>meter:	hundred	thousand	ten
9. <u>demo</u>graphics:	show	people	poll
10. <u>dent</u>istry:	doctor	cavity	tooth
11. <u>digit</u>ization:	finger	switch	number
12. <u>dormi</u>tory:	room	sleep	share
13. <u>du</u>plicate:	two	copy	print
14. <u>frater</u>nize:	club	brother	house
15. <u>libra</u>rian:	help	organize	book
16. <u>mater</u>nal:	mother	parent	matter
17. <u>octa</u>gon:	six	seven	eight
18. <u>manu</u>al:	masculine	hand	book
19. <u>Decem</u>ber:	ten	eleven	twelve
20. <u>litho</u>graphy:	print	copy	stone

Challenge: On your own paper, write a short story using at least five of the words on this page.

Name: _____   Date: _____

LANGUAGE: VOCABULARY ACQUISITION AND USE—
Using Dictionaries and Thesauruses

CCSS.ELA-LITERACY.L.8.4.C: Consult general and specialized reference materials (e.g., dictionaries, glossaries, thesauruses), both print and digital, to find the pronunciation of a word or determine or clarify its precise meaning or its part of speech.
CCSS.ELA-LITERACY.L.8.4.D: Verify the preliminary determination of the meaning of a word or phrase (e.g., by checking the inferred meaning in context or in a dictionary).

Directions: Write a synonym or brief definition for each word. If there is more than one meaning in the dictionary, select the one for the given part of speech.

1. abet (verb) _____
2. audacious (adjective) _____
3. porous (adjective) _____
4. allot (verb) _____
5. sporadic (adjective) _____
6. ardent (adjective) _____
7. embargo (noun) _____
8. enigma (noun) _____
9. revenue (noun) _____
10. mien (noun) _____
11. pithy (adjective) _____
12. onslaught (noun) _____
13. blasé (adjective) _____
14. ferret (verb) _____
15. renown (noun) _____
16. enhance (verb) _____
17. citadel (noun) _____
18. hindrance (noun) _____
19. doctrine (noun) _____
20. assimilate (verb) _____

Directions: Circle the choice that rhymes with each underlined word.

21.	crouch:	botch	couch	enough
22.	assail:	veil	assay	recoil
23.	aloof:	laugh	rough	spoof
24.	comply:	silly	rely	really
25.	cite:	city	quit	polite

Name: _____ Date: _____

LANGUAGE: VOCABULARY ACQUISITION AND USE—
Isn't That Punny?

CCSS.ELA-LITERACY.L.8.5: Demonstrate understanding of figurative language, word relationships, and nuances in word meanings.
CCSS.ELA-LITERACY.L.8.5.A: Interpret figures of speech (e.g. verbal irony, puns) in context.

Directions: Explain each figure of speech.

1. When spring arrived after a long snowy winter, the cottonwoods in the park were relieved.

   _____

2. A sign in the home improvement store window says, "stainless steel sinks." I thought everyone knew that.

   _____

3. What has a tongue, but no mouth, a heel but no foot, and a soul, but no heart?

   _____

4. "We called him tortoise because he taught us," said the Mock Turtle angrily; "really you are very dull!" (Lewis Carroll, *Alice's Adventures in Wonderland*)

   _____

5. A bunch of cowboys were horsing around on Main Street until the sheriff hoofed it down the block to rein in their nonsense.

   _____

   _____

6. "… And in some perfumes is there more delight than in the breath that from my mistress reeks." (William Shakespeare, "Sonnet 130")

   _____

   _____

7. Oh, please assign us more homework during spring break. We absolutely deplore free time.

   _____

8. My younger siblings' antics are so charming, especially when I am entertaining friends.

   _____

9. There is nothing amiss. I always lie on the ground groaning with my left foot facing the wrong way.

   _____

10. Romeo: I dreamt a dream tonight.
    Mercutio: And so did I.
    Romeo: Well, what was yours?
    Mercutio: That dreamers often lie. (William Shakespeare, *Romeo and Juliet*)

   _____

   _____

Name: _____ Date: _____

LANGUAGE: VOCABULARY ACQUISITION AND USE—
Using Word Relationships

CCSS.ELA-LITERACY.L.8.5.B: Use the relationship between particular words to better understand each of the words.
CCSS.ELA-LITERACY.L.8.5.C: Distinguish among the connotations (associations) of words with similar denotations (definitions) (e.g., *bullheaded, willful, firm, persistent, resolute*).

Directions: In the box below, find the word that best completes each analogy. Write it on the line provided. You may need a dictionary and a thesaurus.

> **pleasant, neutral, outbursts, magnate, exotic, instigate, summery, admonition, trade, abound, seize, preposterous, extol, wrong, rational, proficient, effusive, adept, callous, tranquil**

1. *Antics* is to *pranks* as *tirades* is to _____.

2. *Chastise* is to *reprimand* as *commend* is to _____.

3. *Bizarre* is to *ordinary* as *irrational* is to _____.

4. *Audacious* is to *pusillanimous* as *plausible* is to _____.

5. *Disgruntled* is to *contented* as *excruciating* is to _____.

6. *Dire* is to *calamitous* as *calm* is to _____.

7. *Balmy* is to *wintry* as *frosty* is to _____.

8. *Banter* is to *repartee* as *rebuke* is to _____.

9. *Clad* is to *dressed* as *amiss* is to _____.

10. *Elite* is to *privileged* as *accomplished* is to _____.

11. *Embark* is to *board* as *barter* is to _____.

12. *Desist* is to *cease* as *initiate* is to _____.

13. *Formidable* is to *daunting* as *proficient* is to _____.

14. *Gaunt* is to *slender* as *outlandish* is to _____.

15. *Pithy* is to *succinct* as *verbose* is to _____.

16. *Plunder* is to *loot* as *confiscate* is to _____.

17. *Loll* is to *lounge* as *teem* is to _____.

18. *Rubble* is to *debris* as *tycoon* is to _____.

19. *Voracious* is to *avid* as *disinterested* is to _____.

20. *Ungainly* is to *gauche* as *unsympathetic* is to _____.

Name: _____　Date: _____

LANGUAGE: VOCABULARY ACQUISITION AND USE— Academic Vocabulary

CCSS.ELA-LITERACY.L.8.6: Acquire and use accurately grade-appropriate general academic and domain-specific words and phrases; gather vocabulary knowledge when considering a word or phrase important to comprehension or expression.

Directions: On your own paper, write a short definition for each academic term.

1. secession (history):

2. scientific method (science):

3. emancipation (history):

4. atom (science):

5. resistance (science):

6. immigration (history):

7. combatants (history):

8. abolition (history):

9. mitosis (science):

10. respiratory system (science):

11. cell (science):

12. replication (science):

13. proton (science):

14. periodic table (science):

15. molecule (science):

16. element (science):

17. hydrogen atom (science):

18. pH (science):

19. acceleration (science):

20. velocity (science):

21. momentum (science):

22. reconstruction (history):

23. amendment (history):

24. intent (history):

25. segregation (history):

26. contemporary (government):

27. balance of power (history and government):

28. suffrage (history and government):

29. representation (history and government):

30. demographic (government):

Challenge: Create a crossword puzzle with these words. Use your definitions as clues. Crossword puzzle software is available online.

Answer Keys

*Pages where all answers will vary are not listed.

READING LITERATURE
KEY IDEAS AND DETAILS
Understanding the Text (Pg. 1)
1. mountains: national park and loggers
2. She is nervous and afraid he is up to no good. She is shaking and goes to the phone.
3. the cook; He's flipping pancakes.
4. call the sheriff, police, or park ranger

Analyzing Dialogue (Pg. 3)
1. frightened; They are hiding.
2. Martin; He gives orders and glares.
3. Angel; We know what he is thinking.
4. The characters act or feel something before they speak. Examples will vary.
5. Responses will vary.

CRAFT AND STRUCTURE
Using Context to Understand Vocabulary (Pg. 4)
1. thorough
2. absurd
3. amazingly
4. scrubbed
5. humorous
6. exaggerated—overblown words for a trivial subject
7. limerick
8. You can't scrub air.

Different Forms, Different Purposes (Pg. 5)
1. Selection 1: to inspire, Selection 2: to inform
2. Selection 1: elegant poetic language, invention (star-spangled banner for flag with stars); Selection 2: Names of specific people and places, relevant dates, and fact-related vocabulary such as *specifications.*
3. The poem uses rhyme and meter as well as sensory imagery to catch the reader's

imagination, while the factual selection is brief, clear, and to the point.

READING INFORMATIONAL TEXT
KEY IDEAS AND DETAILS
Facts and Inferences (Pg. 9)
1. 1821 (1799 + 22)
2. Beavers
3. To hunt fur animals, especially beaver
4. For coats, hats, and other fur clothing
5. No. "purportedly"
6. Jedediah Smith was a mountain man who explored the West in the early 1800s.
7. Answers will vary, but should include facts from the selection.

Connections and Distinctions (Pg. 10)
1. Did not support it, against his religion
2. To negotiate release of Beanes, a doctor
3. In a sloop, a small sailboat
4. A government hostage negotiator; to help with the talks
5. They were trying to capture Baltimore
6. The British had failed, and the city was safe.
7. No. The flag meant the fort had not been captured, and they had lost the battle.

CRAFT AND STRUCTURE
Building Vocabulary Through Context (Pg. 11)
1. b. computers
2. c. referee
3. a. thousand-year period
4. a. counteract
5. c. unbeatable
6. d. lifespan
7. b. check
8. a. recovered
9. c. base
10. a. fringe

Analyzing a Paragraph (Pg. 12)
1. first
2. to compare the unfamiliar to something familiar, making it more understandable
3. atom, nucleus, shell, proton, neutron, electron, hydrogen, element

4. hydrogen and plutonium
   a. They both are made up of atoms, which have nucleui, shells, protons, and electrons.
   b. Hydrogen has one proton and one electron. Plutonium has 94 protons and 150 neutrons.
5. sentence in parentheses
6. the last

Determining Purpose (Pg. 13)

1. to persuade people to stay off railroad tracks
2. People say tracks are safe shortcuts because they are convenient and seldom used.
3. Tracks are private property and are used more often and unexpectedly than it seems.
4. 500 people die each year walking on tracks; a train traveling 55 mph needs a mile to stop
5. Walking on tracks can be fatal. Trains cannot stop as fast as cars and trucks.

INTEGRATION OF KNOWLEDGE AND IDEAS
When the Medium Looms Large (Pg. 14)

Answers may vary. The following are suggestions:

1. c
2. d
3. c or f: demonstration with models of Earth and moon
4. b
5. b
6. c, d, or e
7. e
8. a or c
9. a or c
10. a, b, or c
11. a, c, or d
12. a or b
13. a, b, c, or a demonstration, if a lab is available
14. a, c, or d
15. a, c, d, or e
16. a, c, d
17. a, c, d
18. d or e
19. a, c, d, or e
20. b, c, d
21. a, c
22. a, c
23. b, f (local newspaper)
24. e
25. a, c, or d

Evaluating the Author's Argument (Pg. 15)

1. Thousands of books stored, inexpensive, out-of-print books available again (can change the print size, Internet connection, research, dictionary feature)
2. Feel of book, no electricity or Internet needed (enjoy cover art, can give a book to a friend)
3. Answers will vary.

WRITING: TEXT TYPES AND PURPOSES, WRITE INFORMATIVE/EXPLANATORY TEXTS
Using Transitional Words and Phrases (Pg. 21)

Responses will vary. Watch for transition words and phrases as well as clear organization.

Challenge: Sequence: after, initially, following, during, preceding, while, throughout, before, whenever, between, since, first, second, third, last, previous, subsequently, for the duration of, finally

Cause/Effect: in spite of, due to, because, despite the fact that, as a result, therefore, thus, moreover, nevertheless, as a consequence, even if, hence

Comparison/Contrast: in contrast to, not only... but also, neither... nor, either... or, whether... or, on the one hand/on the other hand, although, however, all the same

Item/Category: specifically, for instance

Summary: in conclusion, all things considered, in summary, to sum up, all in all

Using Precise Vocabulary (Pg. 22)

1. preceding
2. discord
3. opposition
4. inhumane
5. undertake
6. galvanized
7. rebellious
8. seceded
9. combatants
10. Emancipation
11. unify
12. Reconstruction

Challenge: Synonyms:
Demolish, destroy; acknowledge, recognize; perception, awareness; quell, suppress; incompatible, mismatched; resolve, decide; disgruntled, discontented

Writing Conclusions (Pg. 23)
Responses will vary, but should include all of the facts, restated in the student's own words with title, introductory sentence, and conclusion added.

WRITE NARRATIVES
Orienting the Reader With Transition Words (Pg. 26)
Answers may vary. Possible answers given.
1. before
2. during
3. near/between
4. at first/initially
5. later

Employing Precise Vocabulary (Pg. 27)
1. balmy
2. gaunt
3. ungainly
4. gingerly
5. blasé
6. preposterous
7. avid
8. articulate
9. sublime

LANGUAGE
CONVENTIONS OF STANDARD ENGLISH
Understanding Verbals (Pg. 38)
1. a. Walking, subject
   b. walking, direct object
   c. walking, object of preposition
2. a. were singing, verb tense
   b. had been singing, verb tense
   c. singing, adjective
3. a. was implied, verb tense
   b. implied, adjective
   c. will be implied, verb tense
4. a. to circumnavigate, object
   b. to eat, modifier
   c. To err, subject

Challenge:
invigorating, invigorated, to invigorate; galvanizing, galvanized, to galvanize; dramatizing, dramatized, to dramatize; facilitating, facilitated, to facilitate; illuminating, illuminated, to illuminate; enveloping, enveloped, to envelop; glorifying, glorified, to glorify; deflating, deflated, to deflate; unifying, unified, to unify

Using the Active and the Passive Voice (Pg. 39)
1. a. is illuminated by
   b. is implied by
   c. is neutralized by
   d. is absorbed by
   e. is mandated by
   f. is initialed by
   g. is electrified by
2. a. cites
   b. compels
   c. deflates
   d. deletes
   e. designates
3. a. The office manager deleted those files.
   b. The instructor's son accidentally disclosed the examination questions.
   c. A developer demolished the last historic hotel downtown.
   d. A teenager living near the epicenter chronicled the events following the earthquake.
   e. A dense cloud of noxious fumes enveloped the entire valley.
   f. A local group banned that particular film last year, but it is available now.
   g. A newly elected leader unified the country.

What's a Mood? (Pg. 40)
1. a. resolve
   b. will portray
   c. quelled
   d. would handle
   e. had accepted
2. a. would have
   b. would join
   c. would vote
   d. would be
   e. could overcome

Challenge:
1. a. imperative
   b. interrogative
   c. indicative
   d. conditional
   e. subjunctive

Using the Comma, Ellipsis, and Dash (Pg. 41)
1. Of course, the
2. The plains—not the mountains—were
3. irreversible… just
4. excerpt—as incriminating as it was—could
5. hoped—no I dreamed—you
6. In fact, Kara

7. that..." Abbey's
8. The lake—undisturbed by a single ripple—was
9. Mrs. Johnson, are
10. rubber... and
11. brother, though usually gullible, saw
12. obsession—cleaning up the beach—was

Using an Ellipsis in a Quotation (Pg. 42)
1. a. "The eccentric old man... was actually a respected member of the city's elite."
   b. "Members of the senior class will be there... to facilitate accurate record-keeping."
   c. "In an effort to woo readers, some newspaper articles portray disasters in... detail."
   d. "A lunar eclipse... is easier to view than a solar eclipse."

Spelling (Pg. 43)
Part 1:
1. pedestal
2. self-assured
3. sequel
4. stationery
5. recur
6. hysteria
7. luscious
8. vain
9. facilitate
10. lavatory
11. millennium
12. obstruction

Part 2:
13. porus (porous)
14. advokate (advocate)
15. adjile (agile)
16. inhance (enhance)
17. asimmilate (assimilate)
18. avud (avid)
19. trepudation (trepidation)
20. sporatic (sporadic)

KNOWLEDGE OF LANGUAGE
Creating Effects With Voice and Mood (Pg. 44)
Part 1:
1. expresses uncertainty
2. emphasizes the action

3. describes a state contrary to fact
4. emphasizes the actor

VOCABULARY ACQUISITION AND USE
Expanding Your Vocabulary (Pg. 45)
1. died of
2. sieze
3. waste away
4. authority
5. insatiable, ravenous
6. grumpy
7. regional way of talking
8. infectious, easy to catch
9. inspiring person (in ancient Greece, a goddess)
10. step in, get involved

Speaking of Latin and Greek (Roots That Is) (Pg. 46)
1. self
2. year
3. book
4. arm
5. head
6. hundred
7. body
8. ten
9. people
10. tooth
11. finger
12. sleep
13. two
14. brother
15. book
16. mother
17. eight
18. hand
19. ten
20. stone

Using Dictionaries and Thesauruses (Pg. 47)
1. assist
2. daring
3. absorbent
4. allocate
5. intermittent
6. passionate
7. restriction
8. paradox or mystery
9. income
10. appearance or expression
11. concise
12. attack
13. cool, relaxed, unmoved
14. search
15. fame, celebrity
16. improve, augment
17. fortress
18. interference
19. policy
20. integrate, adjust to
21. couch
22. veil
23. spoof
24. rely
25. polite

Isn't That Punny (Pg. 48)
1. They were re-leaved (got new leaves).
2. Steel is heavy, so it sinks.
3. A shoe—all the parts named are homophones.
4. The "tortoise" sounds like someone who might have taught (in Wonderland, anyway).
5. The terms *horsing around, hoofed it,* and *rein in* all relate to cowboy life.
6. The speaker's girlfriend does not have sweet breath ("reeks").
7. sarcasm: saying the opposite of what is really meant
8. sarcasm
9. sarcasm
10. pun—dreamers often lie (in bed/tell untruths)

Using Word Relationships (Pg. 49)
1. outbursts
2. extol
3. rational
4. preposterous
5. pleasant
6. tranquil
7. summery
8. admonition
9. wrong
10. proficient
11. trade
12. instigate
13. adept
14. exotic
15. effusive
16. seize
17. abound
18. magnate
19. neutral
20. callous

Academic Vocabulary (Pg. 50)
1. separation from the Union, withdrawal
2. a way of learning about the world by forming a question, collecting information through observing, experimenting and testing a hypothesis
3. release from slavery
4. smallest unit of matter
5. a force keeping something from happening
6. moving into a country or area
7. fighters, soldiers, people fighting in a war
8. elimination of slavery
9. A cell divides into two new cells, each with the same number of chromosomes as the first cell.
10. a set of organs involved with providing oxygen to the cells
11. the smallest unit of life, including a nucleus, cytoplasm, and a cell membrane or wall
12. duplication, copying
13. positively charged part of an atom's nucleus
14. a chart showing all of the chemical elements arranged by atomic numbers
15. two or more atoms bonded together, forming the smallest unit of a chemical element or compound
16. a substance consisting of one type of atom
17. has a single proton in the nucleus and a single electron in the shell
18. measure of acidity or alkalinity
19. rate of increase in speed
20. speed
21. force of forward movement and resistance to slowing
22. period of readjustment after the Civil War
23. addition to a law or the Constitution
24. something that was planned
25. the separation of groups of people resulting in unfair treatment
26. current, present-day
27. branches of government hold each other's power in check
28. voting rights
29. members of a law-making body are elected by the people of an area and stand for their interests
30. a group of people sharing certain characteristics such as age, gender, or marital status

Photo Credits for *Common Core Language Arts Workouts: Grade 8*

pg. viii   Heath Middle School Science Project Ongoing at Paducah Site (7609897756).jpg {PD-USGov/DOE} ENERGY.GOV. 10 Nov. 2011. Bomazi. 12 Oct. 2014. <http://commons. wikimedia.org/wiki/File:Heath_Middle_ School_Science_Project_Ongoing_at_ Paducah_Site_(7609897756).jpg>

pg. 4   Old Lady Shapoklyak (Cosplay).jpg {PD-CC-SA-3.0} Dmitry Rozhkov. 30 Sept. 2011. <http:// commons.wikimedia.org/wiki/File:Old_ Lady_Shapoklyak_(Cosplay).jpg>

pg. 5   Fort McHenry flag flying 3.JPG {PD-CC-SA-4.0} Bohemian Baltimore. 24 Jun. 2014. <http://commons. wikimedia.org/wiki/File:Fort_McHenry_ flag_flying_3.JPG>

pg. 6   RJDeath.jpg {PD-Old} H. Parker Rolfe, Philadelphia. 1908. Larry Yuma. 12 Jun. 2006. <http://commons. wikimedia.org/wiki/File:RJDeath.jpg>

pg. 7   Theseus and the Minotaur.gif {PD-Old} H.A. Guerber. 1896. Gunduu. 21 Apr. 2014. <http://commons. wikimedia.org/wiki/File:Theseus_and_ the_Minotaur.gif>

pg. 8   Black cat on window.JPG {PD-Author} Share Bear. 29 Jan. 2007. <http://commons.wikimedia.org/wiki/ File:Black_cat_on_window.JPG>

pg. 11   Baking soda and vinegar.jpg {PD-CC-SA-2.0} katerha. 8 May 2011. Daniele Pugliesi. 10 Dec. 2012. <http:// commons.wikimedia.org/wiki/File: Baking_soda_and_vinegar.jpg>

pg. 12   Elektronskal 94.png {PD-GFDL/CC-SA-3.0} Peo at the Danish language Wikipedia. 23 Jul. 2008. <http://commons.wikimedia.org/wiki/ File:Elektronskal_94.png>

pg. 14   DNA Furchen.png {PD-Author} Yikrazuul. 1 Apr. 2010. <http://commons. wikimedia.org/wiki/File:DNA_Furchen. png>

pg. 15   Kobo ereader touch black front.JPG {PD-CC-SA-3.0} Honza chodec. 5 Nov. 2011. <http://commons. wikimedia.org/wiki/File:Kobo_ereader_ touch_black_front.JPG>

pg. 16   Nuvola 2.0+ Drama.svg {PD-GFDL/CC-SA-3.0} Doodle-doo H. 14 Nov. 2007. <http://commons.wikimedia. org/wiki/File:Nuvola_2.0+_Drama.svg>

pg. 18   Constitution We the People. jpg {PD-Old} U.S. Constitution. 1787. Bluszczokrzew. 3 Aug. 2010. <http:// commons.wikimedia.org/wiki/File: Constitution_We_the_People.jpg>

pg. 21   GoldenSpikev3.jpg {PD-Old} Andrew J. Russell. 10 May 1869. Cave cattum. 14 May 2006. <http://commons. wikimedia.org/wiki/File:GoldenSpikev3. jpg>

pg. 23   Lithium Atom.png {PD-GFDL/ CC-SA-3.0} 56ka. 24 Nov. 2009. <http:// commons.wikimedia.org/wiki/File: Lithium_Atom.png>

pg. 36   Campaign poster for William J. Bryan, 1900.tif {PD-Old} Neville Williams. ca. 1900. Tryphon. 1 Jan. 2014. <http://commons.wikimedia.org/wiki/ File:Campaign_poster_for_William_J._ Bryan,_1900.tif>

pg. 38   Sandwich lunch.jpg {PD-CC-SA-1.0} MarkBuckawicki. 11 Jan. 2014. <http://commons.wikimedia.org/wiki/ File:Sandwich_lunch.jpg>

pg. 39   Hotel Meridian demolition November 2011.jpg {PD-CC-SA-2.0} Nathan Culpepper. 2011. Dudemanfellabra. 5 Jan. 2012. <http://commons.wikimedia.org/wiki/ File:Hotel_Meridian_demolition_ November_2011.jpg>

pg. 40   Abraham Lincoln Vampire Hunter (Cropped).jpg {PD-CC-SA-2.0} Official Navy Page by MyCanon. 12 Jun. 2012. <http://commons.wikimedia.org/ wiki/File:Abraham_Lincoln_Vampire_ Hunter_(Cropped).jpg>

pg. 42   Lunar Eclipse 05.41 UT.JPG {PD-Author} Gestrgangleri at English Wikipedia. 15 Jan. 2010. <http:// commons.wikimedia.org/wiki/File: Lunar_Eclipse_05.41_UT.JPG>

pg. 46   Color1.jpg {PD-CC-SA-3.0} Lecarosamaro. 29 Sept. 2010. <http:// commons.wikimedia.org/wiki/File: Color1.jpg>

pg. 47   Caleb (8021394750).jpg {PD-CC-SA-2.0} theveravee. Magnus Manske. 26 Jun. 2013. <http:// commons.wikimedia.org/wiki/File: Caleb_(8021394750).jpg>

pg. 49   Palm trees tropical beach.jpg {PD-Author} Jon Sullivan. 27 Feb. 2013. <http://commons.wikimedia.org/wiki/ File:Palm_trees_tropical_beach.jpg>

pg. 49   Snow on fir trees.jpg {PD-CC-SA-3.0} christmasstockimages.com. 4 Mar. 2011. Colin Biesterfeld. 13 Nov. 2012. <http://commons.wikimedia.org/ wiki/File:Snow_on_fir_trees.jpg>

pg. 50   Crossword (6857403699). jpg {PD-CC-SA-2.0} russavia. 11 Feb. 2012. Magnus Manske. 26 Jan. 2013. <http://commons.wikimedia.org/wiki/ File:Crossword_(6857403699).jpg>